"Actin' Like Hell"
Memoirs of Judge Acton Cleveland

By Acton Cleveland

With Additional Biographical and Other Information about People and Places Mentioned Herein by Stephanie Korney

Edited by Stephanie Korney

ISBN: 9781730942921

CONTENTS

ACKNOWLEDGMENTS

Special thanks to Leland Pauly (1924-2017) who preserved Acton Cleveland's memoirs and passed them on to the Camptonville Historical Society; Rosemary Wimmer who shared photos of her grandfather Dr. F.K. Lord and her father Otho Lord; Bonnie Wayne McGuire who gave permission to reprint her essay on Judge Acton Cleveland; Clayton Smith, godson of Acton Cleveland, who donated a treasure trove of historic photographs of the Cleveland and Meek families to the Historical Society, and to Leland's nephew Alan Johnson for his donation of Leland Pauly's photographs to the Historical Society. Very special thanks to Rochelle Bell and Rod Bondurant for their excellent proofreading skills.

CHAPTER 1

A WEDDING

Mr. & Mrs. E. L. Cleveland
Married June 1st 1899

On June 1, 1899, a wedding took place in Camptonville; one of the largest and most popular weddings ever to be held in this small mountain community. Earl Leroy Cleveland, age 19, and Lottie Adeline Meek, age 19, were united in marriage by the Rev. Sims, of the Congregational Church of Nevada City.

The bride was the daughter of William Bull Meek, Camptonville merchant, pack-train operator, stage driver, and Justice of the Peace, and the wedding was held at the Meek home on Main Street.

The weather was wet, and so were some of the participants at the wedding. Champagne and other liquid refreshment were on hand following the ceremony and many imbibed (as people usually do when it's free!). The groom stated later on that everyone was intoxicated except himself, the bride, and the minister, and that he thought the latter would like to have had a little snort, but that it wouldn't be appropriate. I doubt this, however, because my Grandmother Meek was not one to imbibe in the spirituous liquid, and I think there were a few more present in the same category.

A good storm had taken place the two days prior and the roads and streets, which were not oiled in those days, were quite muddy, and some of the participants became involved in the mud. Jim Johnson and Bill Jenkins had on their best bib-and-tuckers, and following the wedding as they progressed up the muddy street, their pants started to slip down, and instead of pulling their pants up, to keep them out of the mud, they rolled the cuffs up at the bottom!

Earl Cleveland

The groom was the son of Mrs. Martha C. Langdon of Nevada City. His father, Thomas Cleveland, had been killed when a wagonload of black powder exploded at the powder house in North San Juan. He had a younger brother, Clarence, and his mother took in washing to support the two boys, one age 3 and the other 4, for 14 years until she remarried John S. Langdon.

There was no such thing as a welfare department during those days, and many times the family hardly had enough food to eat, and the boys had to go barefooted because of the inability to buy sufficient clothing or shoes.

As a boy, after school, Earl carried messages for the Western Union Telegraph Company and while engaged in this, the woman telegraph operator taught him the Morse Code and how to dispatch and receive messages.

After he quit school, he went to work for the Nevada County Narrow Gauge Railroad and became an expert telegrapher, taking messages directly from the wire onto the typewriter.

The bride was also an expert telegrapher and held the position as dispatcher at the old Mountain House Hotel, twelve miles east of Camptonville on the old Downieville road, and the two first made their acquaintance over the wire via the Morse Code, and thus the romance started which culminated in their wedding.

John R. Meek
Acton & Lottie Meek Cleveland
William B Meek

On August 4, 1900, at five o'clock in the morning, to this couple was born a ten-pound boy, and that's where I came into the picture. Dr. F. K. Lord, the town doctor and my mother's sister's husband, officiated and told me later that he found me under a cabbage leaf, but even in my extreme youth I didn't believe that.

During the first few years of my life, we lived in various places during which time my father was a dispatcher for the Southern Pacific Railroad, including Hawthorne and Verdi, Nevada, where the sandstorms covered the windows with dust, and the Indians would rub the dust off to peek in and frighten my mother to death.

Later we were transferred to Palo Alto and then San Jose. Little did I know then, when the SP Depot was little better than a box car, that at some future time I would return there to go to school at Stanford University. It was in that station that they had an over-zealous boy working in the office, always pestering the agents for something to do.

To keep him out of their hair one day they sent him all over town looking for a left-handed monkey wrench, and the next day they gave him a purple typewriter ribbon, which they said was "dirty" and had to be washed. Needless to say, the sink and the boy were a purple mess, and that was the end of his being over-ambitious.

While living in San Jose, our home was near a park, and bicycle-riding was quite the style. One Sunday we had company, and my mother sent my father to the neighborhood store for some groceries. Mounted on his bicycle, he took a shortcut through the park, and on the way back, with the bag of groceries in his arm, the bicycle wheel struck a small rock in the path and sprawled him all over the path right in front of a bench upon which an old man was sitting. The old man exclaimed, "Young man, did you have an accident?" My father replied, in a tone of anger, "No, you damn fool, that's the way I always get off!"

Acton Cleveland

We were living in San Jose in 1906 during the great San Francisco earthquake and fire. I was sleeping in a folding bed, and when the earthquake started, I was awakened by the awful noise of pots, pans, dishes, and everything crashing to the floor. The bed folded up with me in it. Moments later, my mother rescued me from the bed, and we all rushed out of the house and spent the next few days in the yard before entering back into the building. We could see the crimson sky over San Francisco, a reflection in the heavens of the fire.

CHAPTER 2

A CAMPTONVILLE CHILDHOOD

Shortly after the earthquake, we returned to Camptonville to live, and from that time on, I became a full-fledged mountaineer, and, at that time, a mean little kid. I was my mother's little Lord Fauntleroy and the apple of my Grandfather Meek's eye. My mother, on stated occasions, dressed me up in knee pants and starched ruffle-collared blouses, much to my displeasure.

Acton Cleveland in Scottish Rite Garb

There was an old Scotch costume in the Meek family that had come down through the ages. Some male member of each generation of the family had to have his picture taken in the outfit, and this fate befell me at about the age of nine. A traveling photographer came to town, pitched his tent studio out in China Town, and my mother adorned me in this Scotch layout and marched me over to the tent for the picture. It turned out okay and was placed in the archives of family portraits, but the whole thing was a painful ordeal as far as I was concerned.

Only one other event at this stage of life caused me more mental strain than the picture-taking event. This was being baptized in the Trinity Episcopal Church in Nevada City. It had to be that church because that denomination seemed to be the one that had descended with the Meek family.

Trinity Episcopal Church

For that memorable occasion, in my Grandmother Langdon's house in Nevada City, I was groomed fit to kill in the very latest, including a set of gold cuff buttons with my initials engraved thereon.

The cuffs on my starched shirt were so rigid that it was almost impossible to get the cuff button through them, and in so doing, my Dad made a dent in both of them, which was not accepted with any degree of happiness by the gentler sex of the family.

William B. Meek

Finally, I was in due form, and we proceeded to the church where all that I can remember of the ceremony was that the preacher splashed some water on my forehead, which I did not appreciate, and that was it. And it was the first, last, and only time I have ever been in an Episcopal Church for any religious function concerning myself. I presume, however, that it did whatever good it was supposed to. All of these things are a part of every well-regulated human being's life, so I assume that it was in proper order; at least done in good faith, and not just to discomfort me.

With my Grandfather Meek, otherwise known to me as "Dado" (which name I will frequently refer to from hereon) as far as my activity was concerned, the sky was the limit. Of course, I was a model child so it cannot be said that he spoiled me; just because he gave me special privileges does not mean that I was spoiled.

He used to take me on many trips in the horse and buggy, occasionally to Marysville where I had the reputation of sitting on the curb at six o'clock in the morning eating ice cream furnished by the only ice cream "parlor" in town that dispensed the famous Peri ice cream, while Dado was in Billy Ward's saloon having what in those days was an "eye-opener."

Peri Ice Cream Parlor, Marysville

Ichi Cohn, a Hebrew man of small stature who owned a clothing store, used to come out and kid me, asking me if I would like to have the ice cream fried.

The Meek family, which started in the mercantile business in 1855, had three store buildings in Camptonville. The first was the old brick store, which was built in about 1852 by another at the cost of $12,000 and later sold to my great-grandfather John R. Meek. This was destroyed in the first fire of 1889, and another wooden structure was built in its place. This was destroyed by fire in 1908, after which the present cement structure was built in its place.

This second building had a high platform for the back porch that was level with the wagon-beds or about level with a horse's back, making it easy to load wagons, etc. At one edge of this platform, an old-style three-holer toilet was in use. Some painting was going on about this time, and I, who have always been artistically inclined, especially with the paint brush, obtained a bucket of white paint and a brush and proceeded to paint all the holes in said toilet. This made it very nice for those sitting on it, at least it was sanitary.

At the same time, a team of horses was tied up to the platform, their backs being level with the same, so I proceeded to paint the rump of the horse nearest the platform, which also was a neat job. And, of course, there were no repercussions as far as my Grandfather was concerned. Not so had my father been in control.

Dado had his own personal horse and buggy and was proud of keeping it looking nice, so he spent considerable time repainting the buggy and putting on the red and gold lines and stripes as all nice buggies in those days had. He finally completed it, and it was a lovely job. In the store, there was a pot of lamp black and a brush that was used to mark and label sacks and boxes being sent out to customers. I procured this lamp-black outfit and proceeded to the shed wherein was Dado's finely painted buggy and went over the whole thing with the lamp black brush to put the finishing touch on it. And a remarkable job I did!

Speaking of horses and buggies, I also had a personal pony and a buggy of which I was very proud. One day a friend from Pike City came in the store and asked Dado if he could borrow the buggy for a trip, and he told him certainly he could use it. I happened to be in hearing distance and came up and told Dado, "I don't want that old son-of-a bitch using my buggy." So Dado remarked, "You heard what the kid said. Guess that settles it, and you can't have it."

Meek House, Camptonville

I frequently used to visit my Aunt Virginia who lived a few doors up the street, and I know that she always welcomed a visit from her little nephew. On one occasion we had a sort of an argument, one of a mild nature, and as she ordered me out of the house, I only kicked over the sitting room table.

There was one good check valve on my youthful life, and that was my father, and leaving all jokes aside, I am very thankful that he ruled me with an iron hand; otherwise Lord knows what might have become of me. When he spoke, I jumped and no back talk. One time before I was of school age, on April Fool's Day, all the kids in the local school played hooky and walked over to Oak Valley with no one knowing where they were. I was not going to school, but joined the caravan without my parents knowing where I was, being so small that the bigger kids had to carry me across the creeks. We were absent all day, and needless to say, my mother was having a real fit because she probably visualized that some mountain lion or bear had swallowed up her little angel.

Acton and His Father Earl

Such was not the case. He returned hale and hearty, but much reckoning took place, and my father gave me the choice of either what he termed "a damn good licking" or to stay in the yard for a week. I chose the latter; it was tough, a whole week n solitary confinement, but the gentler sex who always came to my rescue helped out a little by finding excuses to send me to the store for this, that or the other frequently.

I have always, from childhood on up, been blessed with a marvelous appetite; few things I enjoy better than eating. My father had one rule: that never was I to leave the table with any food left on my plate. Once I had some delicious pie, and I consumed the piece which I had been served and advised my mother that I wanted another piece. She thought I had had enough and that my eyes were bigger than my stomach, but I insisted, so my father said if I took it, I would have to eat it all ,to which I agreed. Consequently, the pie was served, and about half way through it, I sheepishly looked up to my mother who was sitting beside me and said, "Mama, I feel a little bit sick." My dad gave me a look and remarked, "You're going to feel a damn-sight sicker than that if you don't eat up all that pie." As you might surmise, the pie was consumed.

Acton and His Grandfather Dado

I was, of course, a model child; the apple of my mother's eye, my grandfather's little saint, and my father's problem. Commenting on my name one time, he. said, "Acton, yes, actin' like hell!"

CHAPTER 3

ALMOST WATERLOO

At the age of ten, I almost met my Waterloo, and I have thought many times since then, when life did not look like a path of roses, that maybe it would have been just as well if I had. At least it would have saved myself and many others a lot of trouble.

At any rate, at the age of ten in 1910, there was still a China Town in Camptonville to the north of Main Street. In the month of February of that year, they were celebrating China New Year's. My grandfather and I were very friendly with the Celestial inhabitants, and we were invited to partake with them of a feast for the festive occasion Amid the aroma of burning punks and other decorations characteristic of the season, we sat down to a meal with everything one could think of to eat that was obtainable. On the menu was some sort of a fish preparation, and I, with my same characteristic eating ability, had to eat everything in sight. In the process thereof, I swallowed a fish bone. I remember feeling it go down my epiglottis.

About three days after that, at school, I took violently ill and had to go home and continued to get worse and was sick as a horse for several days. There was no doctor here at that time. Dr. Lord had moved to Fair Oaks and opened up shop. My folks phoned to him, and he came back and treated me. I apparently had passed the worst of it and was recovering. They hired a nurse for me, and when Dr. Lord returned to Fair Oaks, he specifically told the nurse by no means to let me sit up, get up, or otherwise be disturbed for a certain length of time. In a couple of days, I improved to such an extent said nurse took the matter in her own hands and propped me up in bed.

It happened that where the fish bone had punctured my large intestine, nature had walled the injured area off and was healing over it, but when she sat me up, she broke down the structure, and from then on, I immediately became worse, and for days I was in a critical condition.

Prior to this I had gone into peritonitis and was filling up with pus. Dr. Lord returned and something had to be done so they decided that I would have to be operated on. Dr. Hydrich from North San Juan, Dr. W.P. Sawyer from Nevada City, and Dr. J.H. Barr from Marysville were all present. Dr. Carl Jones from Grass Valley had looked at me a day before on his way through here to Allegheny to treat a girl my same age who had a similar sickness. They made an operating room out of my grandmother's living room, or parlor as it was then called, and cut me open. All they could do in this setting was to let the pus out and put in tubes to drain.

I was a sad citizen: a hole cut in my belly in two places with a tube between them, suffering like hell, thin as a skeleton, with very little chance for recovery. However, I was determined to live, and the doctor said that it was only my determination that caused me to live, so I struggled on. I became so thin, and with such pain with my legs doubled up, I broke the skin across the top and front of both knees, causing some ten to twenty scars on each knee. which I have and will carry all my life.

They tried to build me up and fed me on melted butter, milk, etc., soaked me in cod liver oil, etc., and I progressed that way for several weeks. I was so bad off that they ceased ringing the school bell and caused all disturbing noises to cease. During this period, O.N. Polley, a brother Mason in Brandy City, died and was to be buried here. The place where they dug his grave was so hard that they had to blast, and naturally I could hear it, so they told me that it was blasting on the county road.

By the middle of March, it appeared that I should be moved in order that I might mend quicker and better. Automobiles were a scarcity, and the roads were hardly fit for a mud wagon. However. Kelly Brothers. then the main undertaking and livery stable people in the county seat, had a limousine that they could send up. There was a huge mud hole in the road between here and Jaynes' so they got a lot of plank and planked over the muddy place, loaded me in the car as best they could, and started on the journey to Marysville. In due time, I reached the county seat and was put up and cared for in my great-uncle Jason R. Meek's home in the old Casey Block on D Street, where the Lipp & Sullivan establishment now stands.

White Hospital Brochure

In due time I recovered so that I could get around a little, very weak and puny and still in the classification of a skeleton. All through that summer I sat around my grandmother's place with my side open and having to be dressed twice a day. Most everything I ate came out my side in the bandages The wound had become calloused and would never heal, so I was taken in the month of November to Sacramento to White's Hospital where a second operation was performed by Dr. John White, a renowned surgeon at that time.

He cut out part of my large intestine, threw it away, brought the ends together and sewed them up, put me back together, and from then on I recovered steadily and became somewhat of a normal individual from then on, excepting that I have had a weak side which I have had to favor all my life, being careful not to lift an strain myself, as some activity might break the whole thing loose, and I would be a mess again.

All of this caused me to lose about two years of school and prevented me from participating in normal activity such as athletics, swimming, horseback riding, etc. I could not live or do like the normal kid of my time. However, I took it alright and forgot the things I could not do and thanked the Lord I was able to survive and live and enjoy the things that I could do.

White's Hospital

We shall now leave me out of this for a while and get into the history of the area, really the main reason for this writing.

CHAPTER 4

THE MEEK BROTHERS

The Meek mercantile business started in Indian Valley in 1855, and in 1866 they moved to Camptonville and purchased the first brick store, which cost $12,000 to build. The store was on the ground floor, with the Masonic Lodge on the second story. The business at that time was known as the John R. Meek Company and was operated by my great-grandfather John R. Meek and his brother, Alex Meek.

Camptonville School 1901

The two boys (Jason and Bill Meek) continued to go to school in Camptonville until they completed all the schooling that could be had locally, which I believe was called the l0th grade and equivalent to the first two years of high school. From what they were taught in this 10th grade, I would say that it might now compare with the whole four years of high school, considering the amount of actual intelligent learning which is taught.

The old folks decided that they would send Jason, the oldest son, to college for a more complete education and keep my grandfather Bill to work in the store and become a merchant. Thus Jason was sent to Montreal, Canada, to attend McGills College, which he did, graduating later as a civil engineer. While there, he lived with some blue-blood cousins who taught the youngster from California all the things that one in good society should know. After he had been there for a while, some still more aristocratic relatives from England were to come visit the Canadian cousins, and with this visit, the very most care must be taken as regards to manners, language, etc., and Jason was heavily groomed ahead of time as to what his deportment must be, which he fully understood. The visitors finally arrived, and at dinner that evening, everything went along fine with good manners, etc. until about the end of the meal, when Jason, the nice boy from California, horrified all present by picking up the finger bowl and drinking the water out of it.

Of course, both boys were model boys when smaller and living in Camptonville. To prove this,, I will cite an instance. They went to church on Sunday along with the other good people of the community, included in which was one Iredell Donaldson Bray, the town constable who was immaculate in attire and habits, always wearing starched, green-checkered blouses with polished cowboy boots, usually with one pants leg in the boot of one leg, and on the outside of the boot of the other. On this particular Sunday, all went to church, and Jason and Bill sat in the pew directly in front of the constable.

Everything was going nicely, along with the saying, as quiet as a church mouse, the sermon progressing, when one of the boys, had gas on his stomach, and with a sharp sound that echoed throughout the quiet building, expelled a quantity there of, and immediately both boys turned abruptly and sharply around and stared at the constable. The constable quietly arose and left the church.

CHAPTER 5

EARLY DAYS

Camptonville was a lively place from the beginning on. When Tom Byrd (whom I will refer to later on) first came to town, he observed 13 fights in front of the saloon before breakfast, a nice way to start off the day! In the early times, people took more time to resort to jesting and antics of fun, sometimes even to the degree of causing disaster. In this instance, I refer to a time when a stranger arrived in town and entered the saloon for a drink.

In the process of getting it, there being a group of residents in the place, they struck up a conversation with the stranger in which they claimed that he insulted one of the citizens, and the only way to settle it would be by a duel.

Therefore a duel was immediately agreed upon. The group was to meet at the old Kendall reservoir site. The next morning at daybreak all met agreeably to appointment, and the usual and necessary procedure for the duel was followed. Each participant was furnished with a six-shooter (the stranger not knowing that they were filled with blank cartridges), Each was blindfolded, took the necessary steps and counts, and turned and fired.

The local man fell, and immediately some of his colleagues poured some raspberry juice on his shirt, making a red spot like blood, and the cry went up, "He killed him, let's lynch him! " The crowd started after the stranger, who by this time had removed the blindfold and started to flee from them, running at utmost speed down the ridge where the Pike City road now winds. He ran out of sight, and the crowd returned joyfully to the saloon, greatly enjoying the prank in which they had just participated.

Nothing more was thought of it, but a couple of days later, someone had occasion to walk down the Pike City Road, and there, to the horror of all, was the stranger's body in the top of a pine tree. Not knowing the country, and running with such fear, he had fallen over the precipice, killing himself, landing in the treetop. Thus a practical joke that was most entertaining to those who conceived it had ended in tragedy.

OREGON CREEK PRECIPICE

The Oregon Creek precipice is a perpendicular cliff one quarter-mile from the town on the Pike City Road. Because of its danger, the county now keeps it fenced. In the good old days it was used as a place for the disposal of useless or dead animals Whenever a horse had outlived its usefulness or had died, it was taken to this spot, shot, and dumped over the cliff. Coyotes, bears, etc. would usually eat the remains at the bottom of the cliff. This same precipice has claimed other victims.

In the horse and wagon days, one Saturday night Isadore Wayman left Camptonville for Pike City for a dance with a wagon-load of young people, and a short way below the precipice, the team started to run away. Tearing down the 35-percent grade, the wagon upset, throwing the occupants over the side, killing Wayman and bruising the other occupants of the vehicle. The hair nets from some of the girls were found in the treetops in the following days.

In later years, Me. Stoddard who lived down Rebel Ridge way came to town to visit and leaving for home late in the evening. He took the wrong street and fell over the precipice. The next day he was reported missing. Deputy sheriffs searched the area but found no one. Later in the week, vultures were noticed circling the area of the Oregon Creek canyon. Constable Louis Marquardt made a search along the creek and found Stoddard's body hanging on a large bush at the base of the precipice.

PLUNGE OVER GRADE FATAL FOR WAYMAN

Owner of Toll Road Dies in Automobile While on Way to the Hospital.

OTHERS LUCKILY ESCAPE

Sacramento Union, April 2. 1911

CHAPTER 6

OUR CELESTIAL BROTHERS

The Chinese race played quite a part in the life of pioneer California. The lust for gold brought them into the mining districts. In Camptonville there were two China Towns; one out in back at the end of Brooks Lane (which was extinct before my time) and the other to the left of Main Street, down back of the present hotel. This one I can recall vividly.

Meek Mercantile in snow 1921

At the time both existed, the Celestial population amounted to about 500 persons, most of them men, although there were a few women. The only one that I can remember was China Mary, who was a short, stocky Chinese woman, with all the garb and characteristics of the Chinese women of that day and age.

I do not recall many incidents of the China Town at the end of Brooks Lane. In fact, about all I remember is one story, which my grandfather told me, being the time when he was just a boy, and in winter his father made him get on the roof of the store and shovel off the snow.

The Chinese from this China Town had to walk out Brooks

Lane and right along side of the lower side of the store building. In the process of shoveling the snow, he would make a huge pile or snowball and fix it right on the edge of the roof. He would then watch out the street and when Mr. Chinaman would come along with umbrella in proper position, just as he walked under the edge of the roof, my grandfather would push the huge ball of snow overboard. It would land posthaste right on top of said Chinaman, squash him to the ground, and break his umbrella beyond repair.

The poor creature would arise, shake the snow off as best he could, and in an outraged manner stalk into the store and "kai-ai" with all his ability to my great-grandfather, who in turn, would rush up through the attic, poke his head out the manhole, and give my grandfather fits for doing it, and my grandfather, innocently, would state that he was sorry about the incident, but he was ordered to remove the snow from the roof, and he did not know that there was anyone, particularly a poor Chinaman, under the eaves of the roof. The whole thing ended by my great-grandfather having to give the enraged Celestial a new umbrella!

For some reason that to me does not make too good sense. It seemed to be the delight of the youth, and surprisingly some of the adults, to try to make the poor Chinese lives as miserable as possible. Along the trails over which they had to pass, the kids used to stretch fine, almost invisible wires, which would trip them as they walked along, and on some occasions, especially in a funeral procession, one boy would get on each side of the sidewalk with a rope and stretch it across the walk, and then both would run holding the ends of the rope in the opposite direction to which the Chinese were coming, causing them all to fall over and pile up on each other.

There was a Chinese cemetery back of and east of Highway 49, up and behind the Camptonville Garage, and a funeral was a big event. Along with all the wailing, the procession from town to the cemetery was a colorful affair with the usual red papers with China writing on them scattered behind the procession to scare away the devil. And a most elaborate arrangement of food consisting of a roast pig with all the trimmings was taken along and placed upon the grave. And after the thing was over, some of the bums around town would go over and have a repast with all the fine food.

In later years all of the bones of the Chinese buried in this cemetery were dug up and shipped to China, and now not a single grave remains in the long forgotten Chinese cemetery.

The China Town which I knew was a colorful place, and I regret that no one at the time had enough sense to take a picture of it. (Of course, in that day and age, cameras were not plentiful). The houses were wall-to-wall together. They were meagerly furnished: crude tables and benches and the beds were bunk type, with a board for a pillow. They never slept with pillows.

In front of each door on the porch was a jar, usually an empty ginger jar, filled with sand in which most all day punks were burning. This also, I believe, had something to do with scaring away the devil. On each front door, in the middle of it, was plastered some red papers with Chinese writing; these were renewed from time to time. In each house a pot of tea was on the table, and one could partake of cold tea at any time of the day. This they drank mostly instead of water or other beverages. Their dishes were purely Chinese, which in this day and age would demand a premium price for the historical value. if nothing else, and of course, knives and forks were unknown, chop sticks being the only implement for eating. (And, I had a hell of a time trying to use them whenever I ate with them, which was occasionally.)

In one fairly central location they had a large barrel buried in the ground, which was more or less a community project, and into which they emptied their urine and other sewage; diluted it with water, and used it to irrigate their gardens. Also, it was not uncommon to see a dead cat hanging on the clothesline, being dried for food at a future time.

These Chinese were of the old country type, wearing long queues and the usual Chinese clothing. They did not speak English very well. In fact, some of them could not talk it at all. My grandfather was fairly well-versed in the Chinese language and could talk to most any of them. And, like any other race, there were good and bad ones. If one of them was a friend, he was really a good one and would do anything for one.

Most of them were honest, although there were a few high-handers in the population. Some of them were in the habit of robbing sluice boxes, and on one occasion, three of them were in process of robbing a sluice box in Willow Creek when the owners came along, catching them in the act, and with a rifle, dropped them dead in their tracks. That is the way justice was sometimes dispersed, and under the circumstances, I don't know but what it is a proper way. At least the state is not out anything for prosecution, and certainly a dead robber will rob no more.

In the early days of my boyhood and prior to the dreaded and senseless Prohibition, most of the liquor locally was sold in bulk. In the back of our store we had what was known as the Whisky Cellar in which was kept at all times two fifty-gallon barrels of two grades of whisky, a barrel of brandy, and one of port wine. The best grade of whisky sold for $1.50 per gallon, and the customers would come after it with either half-gallon wicker jugs or demijohns and buy it in bulk. And I must say here that the quality of this $1.50 whisky was far ahead of anything that we now pay around $6.00 a fifth-quart for.

The Chinese were our best whisky customers. They would come to the store, pigtails waving, in their silk frog-buttoned jackets, with their jugs for their daily refreshment. Sometimes, while waiting on them, my grandfather would give them a cigar as they left, loaded, of course. These loaded cigars had a powerful spring on the inside tied together with a string, When the cigar burned down to the string, it burned the string, and the spring flew apart, bursting the remains of the cigar into smithereens, and scaring the smoker to death. After the poor victim would leave the store, everyone in it would watch him, and about the time he reached the beginning of China Town, the cigar would blow up, scaring him frantically, in which fright he would drop the jug of whisky, it landing on a rock and breaking, and all the precious liquid spilling on the ground. He would immediately return to the store greatly enraged with anger over the incident, and my grandfather, in his good nature, would pacify him, give him another jug of whisky, and another cigar (but this time a good one), and the poor Celestial would leave all in smiles, thinking that Bill Meek was one hell of a good guy.

In my time, we had two Chinese work for us. One. Ah Wong, lived above the store and took care of my grandmother's lawn. As a little kid, I seemed to delight in tormenting him and tried to give him a bad time in whatever he had to do.

When he would cut the grass, I would sit on his rake so that he could not budge it. He would scold me and tell me that he would "kick ass," but he never did it, and he would stand there by the hour until my grandmother would come out and make me get off the rake and leave him alone.

He was a great drinker and half the time was half plastered. One day we had a wagon-load of dynamite arrive, and it was to be unloaded in our powder magazine, which was below town underground beneath a lumber shed. He had a fifty-pound box on his shoulder and was so drunk he could hardly walk and right beside me dropped it from his shoulder to the hard ground floor. For some unknown reason it did not go off. Had it, I would not be sitting here typing this at this moment. He was very kind-hearted and kept me pretty well supplied with fire crackers.

The other one who worked for us for years was Ah Suey, a cook. He cooked for us both at my grandmother's house and at the hotel when we ran it. He could talk a little better English than the average. He could not, however, master my name and called me "Wickton," (which is not too much worse than some Americans have butchered it, Addison, Atkin, Action, Aklin, etc.), and as my father said, "Actin' like hell."

Ah Suey was a good cook. He wore a long que, and once in a while, in the large, light fluffy, raised biscuits he used to make, one would find a que hair curled up in the middle of it. He had the rheumatism, and at one time, paid someone to catch a rattlesnake for him, put the snake in a large fruit jar, and filled it full of whisky, which, of course, drowned the snake. After it cured for some little time, Suey used to take a small glassful each day for his rheumatism. This he kept in my grandmother's cellar for quite some time. It was perfectly safe as none of the other drinkers in the vicinity cared for that kind of high-ball!

I do not recall many of the names of the Chinese I knew in the local population, but the few included, along with the two above mentioned, Rat Eye. I do not know what his proper name was. He had been injured in an explosion and had a crippled hand, and his face was somewhat deformed., He was a good old soul, but could not say a word of English, and it certainly was a chore to try to wait on him in the store.

Then Ah Chung. This one was quite an intelligent person. He lived in a little cabin near Garden Valley. Ah Sing, lived in Garden Valley. He worked hard all his life to get enough money to go to China with, and when he finally accomplished it and left for China with all his money with him; he got as far as Stockton where he was robbed and murdered. Rat Eye was the last survivor of the Chinese population in this community, and after he died there were no more. The old were gone, and no new ones ever came.

Their meager cabins were scattered throughout this area. Here and there in every direction could be found a cabin in some secluded spot near a creek where the panning or sluicing was good, and about weekly or monthly they would come to our store to sell their gold dust.

They were mostly all good honest citizens and did well by the community, considering the half a chance they had with the tormenting and other cruel practices that were played upon them by the white population.

They did have peculiar medicinal habits, using herbs and reptiles. They made medicine from horn toads and rattlesnakes and paid a price for these when caught. One time, one of the Hansons was below town, and in jumping over a log, was bit on the arm by a rattlesnake. It happened right near a Chinaman's cabin, and the Chinaman made him come in, lay down, and be quiet, while he went out into the woods, picked some herbs of some kind, came in, stewed them up on the stove, plastered them on the bite, and within a short time, the victim was able to proceed on home and had no bad results from the ordeal.

Ah Wong was a great friend of Dr. Lord. One night amidst a terrific snow storm, the doctor had a call to go to a sick person in or near Dobbins. He started out on horseback, and in the lower end of town, on a slippery street, the horse fell down, landing on top of the doctor and breaking his leg. Ah Wong was very attentive to the doctor while he was incapacitated.

The first thing he did, he prepared some kind of a black plaster stuff with which he was going to poultice the doctor's leg. On his way into the bedroom, having had one too many, he caught his toe on a rug and went headlong towards the bed. The tin pan with the plaster in it flew through the air and landed in full force on the neat wallpaper in the bedroom. My Aunt Jennie was the doctor's wife, and it is needless to say that her temperament was not any too good at this stage of the game and poor Ah Wong found it necessary to make a quick disappearance.

Then in a day or so, he thought that the doctor should have some outside food, so he proceeded to prepare a chicken for him. He roasted the chicken, all wrapped up in a ball of clay - feathers, guts and all!! And when done, he brought it to the doctor with great politeness. You can guess what happened to the chicken! It is peculiar that my aunt did not appreciate this Celestial friendliness and spirit!

CHAPTER 7

THE GENERAL MERCANTILE STORE

The general store in my town is a place of general gathering, a place of discussion of any and all subjects, sometimes good and sometimes bad.

Meek Mercantile

The general merchandise store was the most important business establishment in every pioneer community, for in it, a person could find practically everything that he wanted, whether it be medicine, clothing, food, hardware, dry goods, horse shoes, or chicken feed. In about 1914, our store adopted a slogan on the tags, letterheads, etc., "We Sell Everything from a Needle to an Automobile," and it was about true. At that time we were selling Model-T Ford cars along with quicksilver, dynamite, whisky, codfish, and about everything one could think of. Our first store was started by my great-grandfather John R. Meek at Indian Valley in 1855. The family came to Camptonville in 1864 and bought out the business, which was a two-story brick store.

I do not remember this too well, although I spent much of my very young childhood in it and had a playhouse in the attic. This was destroyed by fire in 1908 and was rebuilt in the form of a concrete two-story building, which is still the general merchandise store. Thus I was practically born and raised in a general merchandise store, and the fascination for such is still in my blood. There is certainly a great contrast between the store of my childhood and the present day mode of merchandising.

In the "good old days," very few items came packaged and practically everything, referring to foods, was in bulk. All spices were in bulk, black pepper, cinnamon, nutmeg, as well as several grades of coffee, beans, rice, cereal, bird seed, etc. These goods were kept in bins and drawers and scooped up and dispensed in paper bags.

There were practically no restrictions as to what could be sold in those days, and no licenses were needed. We carried in stock and on the shelves several grades of bottled whisky and had it in bulk from which it was dispensed in quarts, half-gallons and gallons! In the drug department, our shelves held pain-killing remedies containing opium, paregoric, etc., which can now only be bought by prescription. Strange as it may seem, the purchase of these items was never abused, and they were bought only when direly needed.

Merchandise carried in those days had quality, whether food, rubber boots, or woolen, and it was sold for quality and not for price. Nowadays, the only thought in merchandising is volume sales, and the almighty dollar. Quality has become a thing of the past.

Grocery salesmen used to come to town and try to sell the merchant their merchandise because of its quality. Many is the time that I have watched them buy a can each of corn, oysters, peaches, asparagus, etc., from our shelves, borrow some dishes from the crockery department, then open a can of like vegetable from the samples they brought and check the quality. And the sale was made on the basis of the quality.

Credit was a tremendous factor in the early day general store. Accounts were large, and many became uncollectable. I have often remarked that if I had the money which my great-grandfather, grandfather and father lost in credit during their years of business I would be wealthy and never have to do a tap of work.

Pennies were unheard of as legal tender in my youth, nickels being the smallest coin used in our establishment. Usually, if an account would come out at, say $125.35, it was the usual custom to drop off $0.35, and if or when the bills were paid by the lady of the house, she was always given a little bag of choice candy in appreciation thereof. Even though we lost considerable by credit, most customers were honest, appreciated the accommodation extended them, and paid their obligations.

There was one customer and one incident in my mind that I will never forget. I will not mention the name because the family is still here, and I would not want to cause them any embarrassment. This man came here from a foreign land, and he wanted to buy a place to settle on. My grandfather took him around in the horse and buggy looking for a place, but none of them seemed to suit him. Finally they came to this one spot, and he looked it over, and it was on the black list too, but as they were about to drive away, he asked my grandfather to stop the buggy, He got out and went a short distance to a small knoll where there were some dry cow manure pads. He kicked several of them over and under each green grass was growing, so he said he would take the place.

He raised a large family on the place and had some sickness in the family which require outside help and credit. My grandfather took him over some items for the house, and food and medical attention necessary for the family. The family was finally raised, during which time our store had reorganized from the W.B. Meek Company to the Meek Mercantile Co., and along about 1925 when my grandfather and I were running the business, the man came in, and I was waiting on him. He informed me that he was going to San Francisco the next week and that upon his return he would pay us the bill he owed us.

I told him that he did not owe us anything, that as far back as I could remember he had always paid cash for his purchases, and there was no outstanding account against him whatsoever. He replied that I was in error and that back some 20-30 years before he owed us a bill of $326.70, and that he was going to pay it. I told him to forget it. There was no such bill nor record of it, and as far as we were concerned, he could forget all about it. He did go to San Francisco, and immediately upon his return, he came in and put the $326.70 on the counter to pay the bill he had never forgotten, and he would not take it back nor take any discount on it. He claimed he owed the bill, and he was going to pay it. This was a display of honesty such as I have never seen before nor since, and I consider this man the most honest person I have ever known.

In my youth, paper money (currency) was an unknown thing in these parts. All business was transacted in gold and silver coin, and there being no bank here during my life, many people buried their money for safe-keeping, and many of the coins, both gold and silver, which passed over our counter, were tarnished from having been buried. When paper money finally showed up, most of the older people were highly incensed as they could not bury it. The dampness would rot it.

The first house I bought to live in after I married was the old P H. Russell home on Main Street. Like most of the old houses it was built right on the ground. The front room had a Boxwood heating stove in it, and directly under the stove was a trap door which was about six inches from the ground. Here, Peter Russell, an old hydraulic miner, kept his money. When he finally became old and began to realize that he was not too much longer on this earth, he called his children together in the front room, took down the stove, lifted up the trap door in the floor and took from the ground $60,000 in $20 gold pieces which he then and there divided up among his family. When I got. the place, I also took up the trap door on said floor, thinking that he might have overlooked something. He did. I found a 25-cent piece!

I was always amazed at what I would term carelessness in the handling of certain types of merchandise in the early day store. Various kinds of poison were on the shelf, the same as cough syrup, vanilla or vinegar. Strong acids used in retorting gold were likewise on the shelf, and in my opinion, worst of all, a box of opened dynamite was at hand on the shelf along with everything else. One day a customer was at the counter displaying a new rifle he had recently acquired, and in the display of if, the thing accidently went off, and the bullet went right into a box of dynamite on the shelf. Why the jar did not set off the dynamite, no one ever knew. People had no fear of such things, and their knowledge of how to handle them, and I guess their good luck also protected them.

One of the most interesting activities which took place throughout the year in the general store was the semi-annual visitation of the traveling salesmen of those days. And they were traveling salesmen in every sense of the word! Most of them traveled with horse and buggy, and for those with a large variety of trunks full of samples, a spring wagon. A few used the stage.

They would come and not stay a few moments, but usually their visits lasted from two to three days to a week. They came one visit in the spring and another in the fall. The merchant had to buy enough stock to last him all winter until goods could be freighted in again in the spring. This meant that all the cellars, warehouses and every space had to be filled with tons of flour, wheat, salt, sugar, barley, bran, etc. Time and space does not permit me to describe them all so I will include only a few of those I thought the most colorful.

A man by the name of Pagnello selling stationery, sundries, and notions was on the road for many years. He knew and could sell his merchandise. This man Pagnello would concentrate for a couple of days on his business and then spend the rest of the week drinking and playing cards at the saloon.

The most outstanding salesmen as far as being characters in my opinion were two brothers by the name of Clark. One was a short heavy-set man who wore a diamond ring large enough to dazzle your eyes. His nickname was Dirty-Shirt Clark. His brother was a tall, skinny, shy fellow whose real name was Frank - his brother's first name was Charley - but he was nicknamed Hungry.

Dirty-Shirt Clark represented the Pacific Coast Syrup Company for many years, selling syrups, preserves, pickles, and a fine line of crockery. As a sideline he sold coffins and caskets, always calling on the town undertaker before he left. Hungry sold a fine line of boots and shoes, gloves, and some items of clothing. Together they had a company selling brooms, lamp chimneys, and glasses, and most every trip they would have acquired some new line in their own company, usually something they had imported from a foreign land.

Salesman's car from 1930, Pacific Coast Syrup Company

Whenever they would arrive in town, Dirty-Shirt would poke his head in the door and yell in a loud voice, "Hello, have you got a big rope in there?" I usually answered him, asking him what he wanted it for. "To tie the bull outside before I come in." Then when he finally got inside tie door, he would start to sing, "Hurrah for the monkey, Hurrah for the Bear, Hurrah for Bill Meek who grabbed them by the hair."

The semi-annual visitations of these two men were well worth the time it took dealing with them and buying their merchandise as the performance and presentation were something that never has been, nor do I believe ever could be, duplicated.

Dirty-Shirt usually brought along an extra supply of fancy crockery samples, and before he left, he always gave my mother a nice hand-painted item in chinaware. I believe he represented the Nathan Dorhman Company of San Francisco for around 40 years until they finally made him salesman emeritus and gave him a pension. Before my time. one of the big events in most all the small mountain towns in the Motherlode was to get these traveling salesmen to become members of E Clampus Vitus. They really got an initiation!

Buckeye Mills

Merchants in the early days had the same grief with customers over certain whims and fancies, imaginations, and superstitions in the old days as they have now. In the old times, there were several brands of flour merchandised in this area.

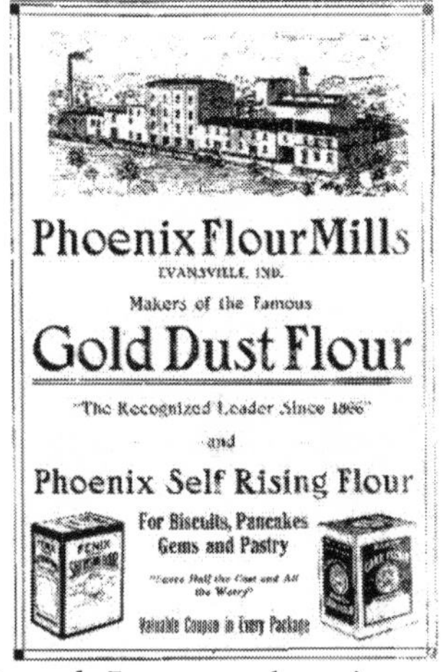

At one time, the Buckeye Mills in Yuba City were destroyed by fire. Our store had a supply of that flour on hand long before the fire. A short time after the fire, a lady in Pike City ordered some flour, so my grandfather sent her some Buckeye Flour.

On the trip after the one which delivered it, she returned it, stating that she had tried to use it, but it had such a taste of smoke from the fire that she could not use it and wished to have it exchanged for some other brand. In as much as it was here long before the fire, my grandfather knew that there could be no smoke taste to it, so he happily received it and re-sacked it in some empty Phoenix Flour sacks - they always kept a few empty sacks of all brands on hand on account of torn or damaged sacks - and sent that over to her.

She was in town quite some time afterwards, and my grandfather asked how she liked the Phoenix Flour, and she replied that it was the best grade of flour she had ever used!

CHAPTER 8

CHARACTERS & PERSONALITIES

Camptonville was a lively place in the early days, and my only regret is that I cannot compile a history of all the old-timers I knew of or heard of as having been citizens of this pioneer mining camp. The same old story: when I was young and had this information at hand, I did not think that it was important; now when I realize its value, I have no access to it. I do, however, have a few things to add to the colorful community of the early days.

PATRIOTISM

Patriotism always ran high here in the early days, and the Southerners at Rebel Ridge were poor losers; they did not say much, but they always had a soft spot in their heart for the Cause of the South and were not very enthusiastic about anything which was against it. The biggest array of patriotism was usually displayed on the Fourth of July; I believe this was true in most all of the early day communities. I can recall when a boy that on the morning of the 4th, just at daybreak, one could hear large reports of exploding dynamite. The old-timers would go a safe distance from town and explode a volley of dynamite, usually setting it off on an old anvil to make all the more noise to beckon in the glorious holiday.

Before my time, the community had inherited an old used Civil War cannon of which they were very proud. They mounted it at an appropriate place on Main Street in front of the old J.P. Brown house. The next Fourth of July, there was much enthusiasm to discharge the old cannon as part of the festivities, and it was duly loaded that morning and a fair crowd gathered to witness it. When it was touched off, instead of firing in the normal way, it exploded and blew into bits, a large segment thereof flying through the air striking a bystander who was instantly killed, thus marring the activities of the day. I had heard his name when I was quite young, but do not remember it.

JOKERS

In the early days, people would go to great effort and expense to play jokes on their fellow citizens, something that one does not see in this day and age. That seemed to have gone into oblivion with the passing of these historic days. The old-timers appeared to have more of a spirit of fun or for fun, and of course, we must realize that they had to create most of their own amusement as there were no such things as phonographs, radios, TV etc. with which to become attached and permit their own talents along such line to disintegrate.

Every so often in our store it was customary to solder a large screw onto one side of a fifty-cent coin and then screw it in the floor in front of the main counter. Then those who were on to it would sit back and enjoy the anxiety and embarrassment of the poor customer who would come in and slyly try to pick it up with no success, then try to pry it loose with the toe of his or her shoe. Sometimes a 50-cent piece would be glued under a showcase lid, and the customer would try to pick it up.

I remember when I was a small boy, William Horwege, known as "Big Pete," happened to be in our store when Joe Stephens, who lived on the old Stephens Ranch near Weeds Point, came to town. In due time, the two became involved in a heated argument, becoming more and more incensed by the moment, when Stephens began to topple. My dad rushed from behind to come to his aid, as he started to fall, my dad caught him, and he died in my father's arms.

After that, whenever I was prone to argue with anyone, my dad would admonish me referring to this incident – that how awful I might feel if the man I was arguing with should drop down dead. And as my grandfather used to always advise me "Two damn fools don't make a gentleman." Most timely, but few adhere to it. In this world, we poor humans must learn the hard way!

There was an old carpenter about town by the name of Trueworthy who was blessed with good philosophy. One day he was sitting on a bench in front of the saloon telling it to a man seated beside him. Trueworthy remarked to his conversational companion, "See that man on horseback coming down the street? "Yes," was the reply. "Well," continued Trueworthy, "That is Sam Johnson, one of the biggest, dirtiest, sons-of-bitches that ever lived, and when he passes us, I'm going to say, 'Good morning, Mr. Johnson' as though he was the best man on earth."

THOMAS JACKSON BYRD

Thomas Jackson Byrd, one of the few old characters I knew, was an interesting figure. He was born in the deep south, Georgia, and came to California while quite young. He told me that the first day he arrived in Camptonville there were 13 fist fights in the main street before breakfast. He called himself a miner, and during his entire lifetime he had never worked for wages but always for himself, and his earnings went from nothing per day up to as much as $1,500. in one day.

His folks in the South were wealthy tobacco people and offered him much to continue on in the family business, but he had the spirit of adventure and was willing to forsake all the promised wealth to come west and do for himself. He was an ardent Southerner and sympathetic of the cause of the South. He settled in the area between here and the north Yuba River towards the west. and in this locality, several other settlers took up places, find they too were from the South. The place was given the name "Rebel Ridge," which name it still carries.

I recall that when I was quite young we had a brass band, known as the Camptonville Brass Band, composed of 18 members, and on Sunday afternoons we used to practice in the large room upstairs of the Mayo Building, the present tavern, and a large number of the townspeople would assemble to hear the music. Invariably, before the practice was over, the bandmaster would have us strike up "Marching Through Georgia" at which point Tom Byrd would always get up and leave the room.

Camptonville Brass Band

His last work here was as caretaker at the old Bullards Bar bridge on the old Marysville Road, a place now under 175 feet of water of the Bullards Bar Dam. He more or less stayed there to look after the bridge for the privilege of living in the house. He had a little store or stopping place on the same road nearer to town before that. He finally decided to go to the Masonic Home at Decoto where he spent the rest of his life, passing on at the ripe old age of 97.

He had never required the services of a doctor during his life. He attributed his excellent health to the fact that every morning when he got up and built the fire in the stove, the first thing he did was to put a small enamel cup of water on, and when the water got hot, he sprinkled some red pepper (cayenne) in it and drank it. He did this every morning and believed that this was one of the things that helped keep him healthy.

THE WHISKEY WOODSMAN

Down on Rebel Ridge there lived a sturdy artisan, a husky woodsman who always kept a bottle of whiskey on the mantle of his fireplace. He had an Irish neighbor living couple of miles distant who visited him frequently, and on each visit, without invitation he would help himself to a drink of whisky, his usual manner being to lift the bottle to his lips and take a healthy slug of it. This began to get tiresome, so one day this woodsman removed the whisky from the bottle and filled it with kerosene, putting it back in the usual place.

The next time his Irish friend called, he went through the usual custom of helping himself to a drink, taking a big gurgle-gurgle. When he took the bottle away from his mouth, he realized that it was not the favorite beverage and started to yell, "I've been pizoned! It's coal oil! How'll I get it out! The advice was, "Stick a wick up your ass and burn it out!"

FRANK LEWIS

I have mentioned that the community had quite a population of Welsh people. They were all very fine, honest, good, hard-working folks and much respected citizens in our midst. Of all the Welsh families one of the most colorful was the Lewis family. Frank Lewis, who was a great friend and admirer of my grandfather, died when I was quite small, so I do not remember too much of him from personal observation, but my grandfather related to me some of the pranks which he played on Frank.

At one time, Frank made a trip to Sacramento, and it happened to be while the state legislature was in session. While there he ventured around the capital and made the acquaintance of a colored flunky or porter about the legislative chambers. While in conversation with his colored friend, the colored man told Frank that he had a dog which was soon to have pups and when this happened, he would send one up to Camptonville to Frank.

This made Frank very happy, and about the time that the blessed event was to take place, he would come in every day and inquire if the stage had brought him anything that day, that he was expecting to receive said dog from Sacramento.

My grandfather was the Wells Fargo Express agent at the time, and he did not believe the colored man would ever send the dog (and he was correct in his assumption), and he could not go on seeing his old friend Frank continually and daily disappointed. Therefore, W B. knew of a family out back who had a dog which was to have pups, so he bargained for one of them, and as soon as the birth had taken place, he obtained said dog, made a wooden crate for it, then plastered the box all over with Wells Fargo labels and stickers, and that night when Frank came to inquire, he told him that sure enough the dog had arrived that day by stage, and there was $3.75 express charges on it.

Frank gladly paid the express charges, took the dog, and was tickled to death. Incidentally, he had the dog all of said animal's life, which was some 12 years, and he always told everybody that this was the dog his colored friend in the California state legislature had promised and sent to him. As a little side comment, I think that the colored man of the legislative body kept his word about as good as some of our present day politicians do, so should we say that the same good old spirit prevails at Sacramento?

Frank also had a riding horse with which he used to go back and forth between here and Pike City; He was employed at the Alaska Mine at Pike; he ordinarily came home for weekends or a lodge meeting only. One day he had the mare bred with another horse and in due time was expecting the blessed event. He had a very poor barn and facilities and besides. my grandfather, among his many other qualifications, was somewhat of a veterinarian. and our family had a huge barn out back of the store which would house almost sixty animals. So Frank asked if he could keep his horse in our stable until after the colt arrived, and naturally my grandfather consented.

Thus Frank brought his mare over to Bill Meek's barn, and

Bill Meek let this event get by without some fun out of it, When the time approached, each time Frank came to town he would immediately come to the store and inquire if the mare had produced the colt yet. W.B. up to that time; each time, said no. Frank was getting impatient, and so was W.B.

So one day when my grandfather knew that Frank was coming home that evening, he prepared a surprise for Frank. He had the horse put in a stall which was rather dark. Then he had one of the boys go out and catch a live jack rabbit. Then he had another go out to the slaughter house which was only a short distance behind the barn and get some blood. He then strew a lot of hay all around the stall, smeared the blood all over it, and had the rabbit at hand. Finally Frank came home, and when he came in and asked about the horse. Sure, my grandfather told him, the colt had been born so they rushed out to the barn to see the new arrival.

As the stall was rather dark, and as Frank approached, he saw the messed up hay, blood etc., and as he peered over the edge of the side of the stall, there he beheld the rabbit. He was naturally somewhat excited, and as he looked in, the first thing he apparently observed was the long ears of the rabbit, and he exclaimed "Damn, Bill, it's a mule colt." It was a few moments before he discovered it was a rabbit, and of course, there was quite an audience in the background to enjoy the joke, and with a volley of laughter and Welsh swear words cussing Bill Meek, the crowd went over to the saloon, and the drinks were on the house - my grandfather as he owned the saloon).

Dave Lewis 1921

DAVE LEWIS

Dave Lewis was a nephew of Frank's and also a fine man and a good friend of mine. He was somewhat of a spiritualist and talked to me much about the spirits.

He had the first taxi business in this area. He bought one of the first cars, a Hupmobile, one of the old- timers with the spark and gas throttle on the dash board. He taxied people all over the country. When he became older, he quit the business and spent the rest of his time as just a man about town, He also died at the Masonic Home at Decoto. I had many funny and pleasant experiences with him and regret that I cannot take time here to relate Will tell of only one .of them.

Many years ago, when the state highways were first being routed in this part of the state, a number of local citizens went to Grass Valley to some sort of a road meeting which started off with a banquet. Dave Lewis was in attendance. When seated at the banquet table, the first course to be served was consommé soup, and it was served in a regular soup cup. and of course, was a clear liquid, beaming hot. Poor Dave, not knowing any difference and not observing anyone else, he immediately proceeded to put a couple of teaspoons of sugar and some cream in it, stirred it, and up and drank it. No comment as he was too polite to say anything, but his expression told the others that to his opinion, that was a hell of a cup of tea!

Dave Lewis was an ardent spiritualist. One could make fun of many things with him, but it was not safe to say anything about his spiritualism as he was very serious about it. In fact, when he taxied the old Hupmobile around, some people were afraid to ride with him on account of the fact that he had a habit now and then of seeing spirits (I speak of this in a veritable manner as he never touched the liquid variety). One day near the Oak Tree Ranch he turned off the side of the road to let an imaginary team of horses pass by.

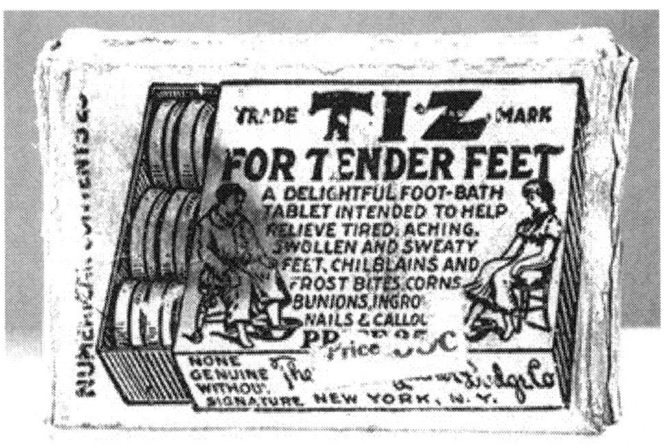

Advertisement for Tiz" Foot Remedy

He was troubled with his feet, so one day someone talked him into trying a patent medicine remedy for the feet. It was called "Tiz" and had a picture of a man on the package soaking his foot in a pan of water with this remedy in it. Dave purchased a box of it, and several days thereafter I asked him if it was helping him or if he was satisfied, and he stated that he thought it was all right except that it took too long to use. When asked why, he stated that a person could soak only one foot at a time, and it took too long. He had taken it that way because of the picture on the package in which the person was soaking only one foot, so that was the way it had to be done.

He had an interesting vocabulary, and in my many years of acquaintance and association with him, I had many hours of amusement. He served as Constable for a short time during which tenure of office fortunately he did not have any exciting situations to cope with. We belonged to a club together, and on one occasion were in a small skit together. We were to "perform" this at

Downieville, so weeks before it took place we practiced until I thought we had our parts perfect. The big night came; we went up there, and when the moment for presentation arrived, he was supposed to have said "Those are the three of whom we are in search," but he became rattled and stage-struck so blurted out, "Them there's the ones we're lookin' for."

He finally sold the Hupmobile and went out of the taxi business. Pete Peterson, the local butcher at the time, bought it. Pete was a big fat man and had never before driven a car, and with the gas throttle on the dash board, had a dashing time. He owned a team of mules used in the butcher business, and his first act with the Hup was to scare the poor mules to death. I don't know what finally became of the old car but thought many times since that it was a pity it could not have been preserved as it would have been a relic worth having and could have been a proud part of the present-day horseless carriage parade.

W.B. MEEK, PEACE KEEPER

My grandfather, W.B., was not a very fat or comparatively large man, but he was a man of strength. His rugged life of driving stage, team, and doing hard work made him that way, and during his time, he could hold his own with the best of them.

One morning about six o'clock he was working in his office when three brothers from out of town arrived out in the front street. There was a stranger, a man of quite small stature who had been in town only a few days, and the brothers proceeded to pick a fight with him. All three pounced on him at once. My grandfather, hearing this, stepped outside, pulled the brothers off, and told them it was okay to fight, but one at a time, so they fought the stranger one by one, and he licked every one of them.

One Sunday morning one of the natives came into our store and was red-hot mad at my grandfather, for what I do not remember. However, as he kept roaring, he became more incensed, and finally drew a big pocket knife and was going to stab W.B. with it, whereupon W.B. emerged from behind the counter and took the knife away from the man, picked him up by the seat of his pants, and threw him down the front stairs into the street. I still have that knife in my possession.

The old saloon across the lane from the store was owned and operated by O.G. Mayo, always known as "Bill" Mayo. He was a great friend of the Meek family, and the present tavern building is named the "Mayo Building" in honor of him. The second Masonic Hall was upstairs of his saloon, and there was a very large horse watering trough in front of the building.

The Mayo

One evening, WB stepped into said saloon and found Old Dutch Jake, a notorious character, in the act of chasing Bill Mayo around the room with a red-hot poker. W.B. grabbed Old Dutch Jake, took the poker away from him, and literally carried him out of the saloon and dunked him in the horse trough in front of the building.

DUTCH JAKE

Of all the characters in Camptonville, without doubt, old Dutch Jake was one of the foremost. He came here as a young man from Shasta County. Little is known of his past life except the stories he himself told, and he was such a liar that one could not believe anything he ever told.

He was born in Germany and said that he had studied to be a priest, but that he was so damn mean they kicked him out, so he came to America. He said that he had been an Indian Scout in the Army and was with General Custer and escaped Custer's Last Stand, all of which we know could not have been true for no one escaped from that!

Had he been in the government service to that extent he would have been entitled to a pension, which he never was, so that fact discounts all the yarns he told about fighting Indians. He might have fought them, but not in the capacity of a soldier.

He always wore a heavy beard, and his hair was usually long. That is, he had a haircut and shave once a year. Some neighbor or friend who owned clippers went over him from stem to stern, face, head, and all, once a year, and clipped him as clean as a billiard ball. This was done in the spring, and by the following fall, it had grown out, and by spring it was a good crop that had kept him warm all winter.

He was one of the heaviest whisky drinkers I have ever seen. He would always come to town with a gallon demi-john, and many times, he would start up the hill towards home and get only part way, lay down, drink the rest of the jug, go to sleep or pass out and lay there in the gutter until the next day. I have seen him do this in the wintertime when the water from the street would run through his whiskers and, mixed with snow, would freeze, but he always survived, and I don't think the man ever had a cold in his entire lifetime.

This would be a perfect advertisement for whisky as an anti-freeze for the human body, but this was offset by the fact that Mark Crosse, another notorious drinking man; started for home one day with a snoot-full and sat down under a tree to rest and froze to death.

Dutch Jake was a fiend for slot machines. I have seen him in the days of the one-armed bandits stand in front of one all day long. The minute he got a jackpot he would put the whole thing back in it. It did him no good to win for the winning sent him back into the thing each time.

DUTCH JAKE AND ANDY MASSA

Dutch Jake and Andrew (Andy) Massa were great friends and

drinking partners. And they liked to play slot machines together. On one occasion, they were in the heat of a contest with the one-armed bandit, and old Jake hit the jackpot and nickels started to fly all over the place. Andy made a grab for a handful, and Jake made a grab for Andy, and after considerable struggling, the only way Jake could get the best of the situation was to get Andy by the ear. He twisted it so hard he almost tore it off, and they both landed on the floor and had to be separated by a bystander. Jake claimed his nickels, and in his usual manner, put them all back in the machine.

On another occasion, a man with a shady background was supposed to have burglarized Andy's house, so he signed a complaint against him The man was lodged in the county jail, and in due time, a preliminary hearing was scheduled, which was held in the old IOOF hall.

The D.A. presented the case, and Jake was the main witness. He walked with a cane and first broke the silence of the proceedings when, before taking the witness stand, he dropped the cane to the floor. Being hard of hearing, instead of giving a direct answer to the D.A.'s questions, he went on with almost a complete story on each interrogation.

One of the exhibits in the case was a six-shooter, and when it was presented, Jake hobbled over to the window and scrutinized the firearm and identified it by showing a mark he claimed he had made on said gun for identification purposes at an earlier date. The defendant was bound over to Superior Court, convicted, and sent to prison. The entire center of attraction was old Jake.

He mellowed considerably during the later days of his life and finally became almost blind and had to be taken to the county hospital where he died. He was a county indigent when he died, and a friend from Sacramento came forth and paid for his funeral so that he could be buried in Camptonville, and I preached his funeral. After the service was over, and the casket was lowered into the grave, Giacomo Cartasso, who attended, approached the grave, looked down into it, and in a solemn manner, remarked, "That's the end of Old Dutch Jake, body and soul."

ANDREW MARTIGNONE

Andrew Martignone who had a ranch in Oak Valley and grew garden truck which he sold to the mining camps in the vicinity, delivered vegetables to Brandy City. His son Marion, a burly youth at the age of 10, helped his father and frequently took the pack train to Brandy City with produce for the camp. It was the boy's custom, after he had disposed of his load, to enter the saloon, call up all the miners who might be around, belly up to the bar, and buy the house a drink. Pretty good for a ten-year-old kid!

GIACOMO CARTASSO

The story of Giacomo Cartasso is one of interest. I regret that I do not know anything about this man before he came to Camptonville. No doubt the story of his life from birth in Italy would be interesting. He came to Camptonville in the heat of the Depression around 1930.

I understood that prior to that time he was a man of means, owned a good men's clothing store in Oakland and was prosperous. Like many, he put the bulk of his savings in Transamerica or some such stock, and when the Crash came, he lost everything he had, including his business.

He had a Model A Ford Sedan in which he loaded everything he could from the stock of his store and came to Camptonville. The reason he came was that he knew another of his native countrymen and thought that through his aid he would be able to dispose of the merchandise in his Model A and probably be able to establish himself in some way or other here.

He peddled his clothing from house to house and got rid of most of it. Then he selected a place in the forest up behind the Zerga place near Oak Valley and established himself a home. There was water there and a sawmill not too far distant. He got slabs from the sawmill and put himself up a dwelling. It was a peculiar-looking structure, with a very steep roof and part of the building underground. It resembled something one would see in Europe and nothing like you would expect to find in America. He planted himself a vineyard and an orchard, which after a period of years, bore fruit.

He struggled on as best he could, and at first, it was very difficult even to get by. About that time, we had a hard winter with considerable deep snow. He struck out one day with rifle in hand to look for game. He had been hungry and without much food. He was also disheartened and melancholy, realizing the plight he was in. He always carried one extra shell in his gun and thought that if worse came to worst, he could use it on himself and end it all

This day he wandered into the forest the snow was deep, and after a few hours, he became lost. He shot his gun thinking someone would hear him and rescue him, but no one did. He finally took shelter under a tree and was going to end it all with that last bullet, but he had miscalculated and shot all his shells in quest of help and so now could not do away with himself. After a couple of days someone passed by his place and missed him so a searching party of neighbors gathered and followed his tracks and found him in a dazed and frozen condition under the tree. They took him home and in due time he recovered from his ordeal.

After a few years, he was able to get what is known as old age security from the county. It was not very much, but it was more than he had been used to since coming here to live. He told me that up to this time he had had to live so conservatively that for five years he had not tasted butter. After he started getting the monthly check from the county, he considerably bettered himself, improved his property, and took quite a prominent part in the life of the community.

He had acquired quite a philosophy of life and could talk fluently on religion and government, He was not much in sympathy with any religion. He had been raised a Catholic, but highly condemned it along with other and different faiths.

For a time, he had another Italian living with him. I never did know the man's proper name, but Cartasso called him Martin. He helped about the place, tilling the soil, getting wood, etc. He complained of having something wrong with one arm and said that he was unable to use it.

He complained so much that Cartasso became vexed with him and one day, he took Martin out into the woodshed, took the axe, laid Martin's arm on the chop block, and was about to proceed to cut it off, saying that as it was no good and useless, then the proper thing was to dispose of it and cut it off. Martin became so frightened, believing that Cartasso meant to whack off his arm, that he immediately started to use it and used the supposed lame arm the rest of his life.

Giacomo was a man of considerable physical strength and endurance. He did not have a horse for plowing, so hitched the plow to himself and plowed up his place. He was a good citizen and neighbor and went about town cutting grass for people and doing other chores.

One time he volunteered to plant our back yard in some horse beans, so one day he dug some trenches about 18 inches deep and planted the bean seed. When it started to come up, he went into the woods, cut a quantity of willow poles and staked them in the furrows to hold up the bean plants. The only trouble was he planted them right under my wife's clothes line so that anything hanging on the line would tangle with his poles, and the whole thing had to be removed.

He spent much time gathering mushrooms in the woods, and he prepared a sort of gravy with mushrooms, which he put up in jars, and also pulverized some of the mushrooms when dry. He was liberal in giving his friends some of these items which he had prepared.

After he became a little older he felt that it was too much work to maintain the place he had made from scratch in the forest, so sold it to an Italian friend from Reno by the name of DeMartino, and he went back to the city to live with some of his relatives. He could not assimilate himself back to city life, so in due time, returned here and lived again in Oak Valley near his former place. Soon a place appeared for sale in town, and he decided that he wanted it. Some of his relatives had helped him financially to get it so he appeared in my office to purchase said place, the price being $2,500.

Without any further ceremony, he took down his pants and from a money belt attached to his bare skin he took out $2,500. in currency and plunked it down to pay for the place. He lived there for several years, produced a fine garden including several varieties of flowers and frequently would bring his friends a nice bouquet of sweet Williams or whatever he had in bloom. He took part in whatever happened in the community, never missed a funeral, and always had considerable comment on the sermon.

Although I have never held a golf club in my hand and know nothing about the game, at one time golf trousers were quite the rage, and to keep up with the times I had a tweed check suit with a pair of golf pants as extra accessory (which I had worn from time to time on select occasion). I also had a red check mackinaw coat and other items of clothing, and one day while we were running the store, I being behind the counter, the front door opened, and lo and behold what did I see?? No one more or less than Giacomo Cartasso, Esq., bedecked in my old pants, my mackinaw coat, and some other items!

Without my having been consulted, my wife had cleaned house and had made Giacomo a present of these items which he wore for quite some time. The poor old man was a good citizen, Would that we had more like him.

He finally had a stroke and died in the Miners Hospital at Nevada City in 1958 and was buried by his family at Oakland. When he was here the first time, he purchased five lots in he local cemetery to be used for himself and his family. As time went on, he realized that he had overbought so sold one of them, and after his demise, the cemetery district bought the rest of them from his heirs.

CHAPTER 9

THE COUNTRY DOCTOR

Dr. Frederick King Lord, the country doctor, and a freer or more typical character of the country doctor could not be found. He was my uncle. He married my Aunt Virginia.

Frederick K. Lord

He had been married before, and our family did not approve of the marriage, but as usual, the family could have nothing to do about it. To this union was born a daughter who died at birth, and later, a son, a very fine man who became a mining engineer.

Leaving aside the aspects of his married life – whether good or bad - whether the family like it or not – it culminated in disaster and was unfortunate. The doctor's worst failing was drinking. It did not effect his medical ability for, to a man in Camptonville, it was said they would rather have Dr. Lord drunk than any other doctor sober.

Like all small town country doctors, he had his office in his home in a front room with the appropriate sign on the door: "Dr. F. K. Lord, Physician and Surgeon." Inside the door was his operating table, his writing desk, and a table on which was spread his variety of instruments. Toward the rear of the room a large screen was in place. Behind it was a sink with cold running water, a drain board, and a work table. Adjacent were several tiers of shelving upon which a variety of bottles, jars, etc., which constituted the doctor's medicines and drug supply. Drug stores for prescriptions were unheard of and all country doctors had to prepare their own prescriptions and medicines. After a diagnosis, the doctor would sit behind the screen and put up the medicine for his patient. As a nosy kid, I spent considerable time around the doctor's office and pretty well knew everything he had in it.

For transportation, Dr. Lord had a horse, which he drove with a buggy and also used as a saddle animal. He kept the same in a small barn behind his house. The doctor was available at any hour in the twenty-four and never did he ever refuse to administer to anyone whether he ever got paid or not. Money was secondary.

He had consecrated his life to suffering humanity and being paid for his services was an afterthought. By day or night, in the heat of summer, in the blistering snow of winter, on foot, by horseback, wagon or buggy, the doctor went to where he was called.

As a boy, I watched him do minor surgery in his office, such as cut out a piece of steel from a miner's hand, open a felon, etc. For the minor surgery, he froze the area before he cut so that it would not hurt. On one occasion, he amputated a man's leg in his office (Elmer Stark Robinson Hall) who had his leg badly mutilated when a two-horse team ran away down Main Street.

The doctor frequently removed tonsils. For this he had an instrument made of German silver which to me resembled a mole trap. He would insert it into the mouth and throat, and when in the proper place would pull a lever and whack! Out came the tonsil or the pair of them. Then a little medicine on the place, and the patient went about his business. The charge? Oh yes, the big fee of $5.00 for a tonsillectomy!

Dr. Lord covered a wide area of service. Along with the Camptonville territory, he went as far southwest as Oregon House and Dobbins. On one occasion. I recall he was called to see a sick woman in Dobbins (Mrs. Bertha Phelan). I do not know the nature of her ailment, but five other doctors were called from Marysville, and they and Dr. Lord went into consultation. The findings were that there was no way to save her. She was on her way out. Dr. Lord told the others of a severe treatment which might bring her through, or on the other hand, it might promote her death sooner. The five others would have no part of it, but Dr. Lord excused them, and upon the confidence of the family, he gave her the severe medicine and she pulled through. He had saved her life, a fact which she always admitted the rest of her life.

Dr. Lord would stay with a patient. If he went to one house, and the patient was very ill, he stayed right with him, whether all day or all night, until improvement was shown or the end came. I have always held great respect for Dr. Lord. He was a man of understanding with a very kind and sympathetic nature, one of great sympathy, and truly a great doctor. It was a sad day for me when he and my aunt had their trouble, and he left Camptonville. It befell my part to pack all his office equipment, medicine, etc. and ship it away.

After leaving Camptonville, he served as a captain in the First World War and won medals for his bravery and service to his country. Following the war, he set up a practice in the little town of Ceres in Stanislaus County where he became well known and revered in his profession in that place. He married a woman from Virginia and lived in Ceres to an old age when he passed away.

Dr. F.K. Lord in WWI

A few other doctors came to Camptonville after his time, but none as good as he. Finally, with the advent of the automobile and good roads to larger places, it became hard for a doctor to maintain a livelihood in the little town.

In order to keep the last doctor there, it became necessary to make up a list of families and individuals that would pay so much a month, for which monthly fee he took care of them without further charge. This was the first example of socialized medicine, which it truly was, but soon the doctor went to greener pastures, and there has never been a doctor in Camptonville since.

Impressed by the service to humanity as given by Dr. Lord, I decided I would like to be a doctor. Prior to my entrance to Stanford University, it was necessary that I have a physical examination, and I went to a we-known Marysville doctor, a lifetime friend of my family, and in the course of the examination, he asked me what I was going to study, and I told him medicine.

He immediately started to talk me out of it. I could not understand it and asked him why, telling him he had been a successful doctor all his life. His argument was this: Yes, he had been a doctor, but now things were different. When he first started to practice, a patient would come to him with a minor ailment, he would diagnose the cause, give the man some medicine, and the man usually responded and received, all at the charge of $25.00.

He continued that in this day the newly graduated doctor would start his practice, must have a fancy office. a nurse, a fancy car, an expensive home, belong to all the service clubs, etc. and that some patients with the same type of ailment would come, but instead of the $25.00 cure, a more complicated diagnosis would be pursued, and the man must have an operation at the cost of maybe $500.00 rather than the $25.00 he prescribed. His reasoning held logic so I gave up the idea of being a doctor!

CHAPTER 10

RELIGION

No story of any kind, historical compilation or otherwise, would be quite complete without touching on the subject of religion. I very much regret that I do not have available, either by virtue of historical document or memory, much material concerning this subject. Without doubt it had its great influence upon the early-day population, but nothing that I can find has been written on the subject.

During my childhood, there were no regular churches here. The only thing that resembled one was a building on Spring Street next to the present hotel known as the Good Templars Hall where an occasional traveling minister held services.

Crystal Truth Club

When I was around nine years of age, Mrs. Olive Groves formed what was called the Crystal Truth Club composed of children about my age, and we held meetings, and the whole thing was patterned after or along with the Unity faith. I was secretary of.

Seems like I became secretary of everything I ever belonged to (next from that of the Nevada City Boys Scouts; Camptonville Fire Department; Gravel Range Lodge; Superior Calif. Judges Association; Camptonville Cemetery District, et al.)

In 1912, when Labadies bought the hotel, they soon bought this Good Templars Hall, tore it down, and sunk a well on the spot, so that was the end of that.

Occasionally, a traveling minister or sometimes one from Nevada City would hold services in the then IOOF (Independent Order of Odd Fellows) hall. Seldom did he have such an opportunity so would make good use of the it in the way pf preaching, and if one would stand on the store porch, one could hear the sermon as well as if he attended it. These meetings or services were usually brought about by some newcomer to town who became overwhelmed with things and imported said minister for such occasions.

The Catholics, of which were a considerable minority, used to have their Masses, but these were held at the homes of some of the members of that faith. About once a month the priest would come from Downieville or Smartsville and have Mass in the various localities: at the Ramm home in Oak Valley, over to Long's Ranch in Slate Range, down at Kelly's place in Moonshine, at the hotel in Camptonville, at Sleighville House, at Joubert's home at Depot Hill, and a few other places.

There were, however, in the very early days a few church buildings here, but I have no proof or record of them. Rev. Gage was one of the first school teachers, and he held services on Sunday. He taught school here for a long time and was a prominent citizen. His grandson, Warren D. Allen, was the noted musician and Director of Music at Stanford University for many years.

There was at one time a Welsh church. The early-day population was composed of several Welsh families, their ancestors having arrived here from Wales. This was located between my present home and the old IOOF cemetery. Services were held regularly. The ministers for said church would come and go and were more or less of a circuit nature and while here would visit the outlying population in an endeavor to gain followers for the church.

There was one here during the time of my great-grandfather, who in the course of his activity visited Mrs. Romargi at Nigger Tent in an endeavor to convert her. The ladies of the town heard of this and were greatly offended and at the next Sunday service they brought up the matter in an endeavor to get the minister put out of town for associating or even visiting Mrs. Romargi.

In the heat of the matter, one of the male members of the congregation spoke and stated that he thought they were acting quite hastily, not giving the minister a fair trial, and that before any judgement was pronounced against him a committee should be appointed to make a full investigation into the charges. They even had investigations in those days! This seemed to be a good idea so a committee of seven was named, seven outstanding men of both the church and community, to go up to Nigger Tent and ascertain just what said minister had been doing there. My great-grandfather

John R. Meek was a member of the committee. The committee secretly sent Mrs. Romargi advance notice that on a certain day they were to call on her place of business, so she prepared for them an elegant dinner and perhaps what in this day and age we would refer to as a "cocktail hour." The committee made the investigation and at the next Sunday service gave their report.

In the report, they stated that they had made a full and complete investigation and inquiry into the activities of said minister and that they felt the ladies of the church owed the minister a complete exoneration and apology, that his activities at Nigger Tent were purely religious, that he had done nothing wrong, and that his only activity in such a place was spreading the Gospel. The ladies should be ashamed in distrusting this man of God in this manner. Whereupon the women were very remorseful, gave the minister a full sheet of forgiveness, and asked his pardon. He thus became a hero rather than a culprit, and like all things, it had a happy ending.

Needless to say the committee had a hell of a good time at Nigger Tent, and what a nice change from the strain and stress of the world, even in those times!

Once in a while, a traveling evangelist would come by in horse and wagon and stay a few days, usually preaching his particular kind of religion in a tent, but this sort of thing was not too prevalent, due mostly to the fact that the population was not large enough to make it worthwhile.

I cannot explain why, and I do not know whether or not this ever was applied to other localities, but in Camptonville, there has always seemed to be a sort of religious connection with the office of Justice of the Peace. Not for any religious meetings or ceremonies, but for the conducting of funerals. I have associated this with said office, but on second thought, maybe it should be associated with the person who held the office. My grandfather during his time buried 109 of the local people, some while he was judge and others while he was not.

When I came along and inherited the judgeship, along with it came the duty of funeral service, and so far I have, to the best of my ability, said the last religious rites for 35 of my fellow citizens. My grandfather had a little English prayer book - part of our heritage from England and the regular religion of the family on the Meek side was Church of England, otherwise known as the Episcopal Church wherein I had such a hell of a time getting baptized, the first, last and only time I was ever in church. He used this little prayer book for all so it was not such a chore for him.

When I came along, however, I did not feel that one book or the same sort of thing would do for all, so whenever I have been asked to perform a service, I have composed a different service for each individual. This indeed made a lot of work and took much of my time, but I have always felt that it was worth it because no two people should be treated in the same way, at least that's my opinion. I have a record of each of these services in my file. I have buried all denominations, Catholics, Protestants, and even an atheist.

Methodist Church c. 1947

There was one man here for many years, a very bright intelligent person who had a marvelous mind for memorizing poetry, philosophy, quotations of great men, and he did not believe in any religious faith. I knew that some day I would have the task of giving the final rites for him.

I realized that it would be mockery to-do this in a religious manner such as was accorded the others. so ahead of time I sent to the State Library for books on the life of Robert Ingersoll, the noted atheist, and I read these writings and took out enough of his thoughts to prepare a sermon suitable for a man who did not believe in God, but did follow the Ingersoll teachings. When this man finally passed on, I gave a sermon which I believe he would have enjoyed. At least it was not hypocritical and was true to his nature and belief.

The first real churches to be built here in my lifetime were in about 1947, both the Catholics and Methodists built regular churches on Spencer Street almost across the street from each other.

St. Francis Cabrini Catholic Church

After these buildings were finished and services conducted therein, I naturally thought that this would put an end to my services in connection with funerals, but such was not the case I continue to act in that capacity, conducting the same either at the cemetery or in the Masonic Hall, and I conducted one service in the Methodist Church.

Even after these two religions were established with a house of worship, they have not been too highly patronized. I think that the reason has been, first, that there is too large a variety of religious belief here to concentrate it into one faith, and along with this fact, there is a certain percentage of the population who have fraternal affiliations which they consider to take the place of a religion, and in as much as I understand there are some 275-odd varities of religion, and no one knows which one is THE one, possibly they are right. If a member lives up to the exact teaching of his or her fraternal order perhaps they would need no further spiritual teaching or guidance, but the hell of it is only a small number of them, as well as a small number of church attendants, really endeavor to live up to the teachings or act like Christians, follow the Ten Commandments or the Golden Rule as to do unto others as they would that others would do unto them.

In the early day China Towns in the community, perhaps their religion was the most memorable, whether right or not, most of them lived up to it. At New Years time - their New Year came in February - they saw that all their bills were paid, and they owed nobody. That's more than their white-skin brothers (many of them) did. They burned their punks to keep away the devil and piled fine goods on the graves of their deceased rather than flowers, most of which was eaten up by tramps or animals.

The white man said, "Why you put food on grave? They no come up and eat it." And the Chinaman said, "Why you put flowers on your graves? They no come up and smell it."

They have a point there!

There were in the area, living intermittently between Indian Hill and Camptonville, the three Bliss brothers. Chester A. Bliss served for a time as Justice of the Peace.

Charles Bliss one day slipped his hands under a board set for a trap for rabbits and was severely bitten by a rattlesnake, which sprung the trap rather than a rabbit, from which he died in a few hours. It was said, however, that whiskey killed him more so than the snake bite because soon as he was bitten some of the neighbors poured a quantity of whiskey down him, which stimulated his blood, rushing the snake poison to his heart.

The third brother was Richard Bliss, known as Dick. He was an atheist, a devout non-believer in God or anything else. From Indian Hill, he moved to town where he became very ill and called Dr. Lord to take care of him. He became so bad with water coming from both feet that he had to put each foot in a waste basket and maggots were crawling from sores in his legs. He suffered the agonies of hell and wanted to die, but for days, he suffered. For some reason, he would not die. Finally, after denouncing God all his life, and when his suffering became so intense he could bear it no longer, he remarked, "Well, I must have been wrong all the time. There must be a God that is keeping me alive." Within fifteen minutes after he admitted this, he passed away peacefully.

CHAPTER 11

THE JUDICIARY

Yuba County Courthouse

My only regret is that I do not have a complete history or story of the local office of Justice of the Peace from the beginning up to and including the present time. That would be a story that would make a book all by itself.

In as much as I do not have this information I will be able to compile only a small amount covering only a brief period of time in the past one hundred years.

I have no records of the early day activities. The only old book I have is the docket which covered a period in the late 1800s. I do not know what happened to the other old dockets, but presume like everything else in Camptonville, they were destroyed in either of the two fires which consumed the town. I do not remember the names of any of the judges in the pioneer days and can recall only a few incidents concerning them.

One of the old timers n pioneer days was going out the trail to Oak Valley on horseback one morning and on the way was met by one of the local citizens, and as they met, the citizen asked the judge where he was going. The judge replied, "I'm going to Oak Valley. Bill Smith kicked his wife in the ass, and I'm going over to look into it."

Another incident involving an early local judge happened when the stage between here and Marysville was held up by a robber. The gunman appeared from the brush and stopped the stage. There were seven passengers aboard. The local judge was inside the stage, When he saw what was going he poked his head out of the stage and said, "As Justice of the Peace of Slate Range Township, I command the law." Hereupon the bandit took a shot at him, and missed him but killed a colored lady passenger inside the stage.

There were three judges in my family, one in each generation. My grandfather was the first. In fact he served at two different times. Following him the first time my father served for many years, then he gave it up, and the office was held by a few others. Then as an economy move, the Board of Supervisors conceived the idea of consolidating all of the seven townships and making only one, which they did, Marysville Township for the whole county,

Judge Acton Cleveland

This was tried for a few years, but did not work and caused much expense and hardship upon the people. So the Board again considered the matter and made another change, this time creating three townships: Marysville, Wheatland and Camptonville.

When this was done, my grandfather was appointed Justice of the Peace and held the office until 1932 when, because of ill health, he felt it necessary to resign, and the Board appointed myself in his place. I continued thus as the third Justice of the Peace in the family. Later on in 1949 when the court reorganization amendment was adopted by the voters of California, the office of Justice of the Peace became extinct, and the modernized office of Judge of the Justice Court was established, which office I still hold.

One of the most important duties of the office in the early days was that of Acting Coroner. On account of the long distance to the county seat and the difficulty of slow travel, when an undetermined death occurred it was impossible for the Coroner to come all the way from Marysville, and for such occasion the law prescribed that the local Justice of the Peace could act for the Coroner, and a fee was prescribed by said law for the same.

As for myself, I have only so acted twice, and on one of those occasions for the County of Sierra, the latter being in the case of a man becoming deceased in a cabin over near Pike City during a terrific snow storm. I had the Pike City mail carrier, a characteristic man by the name of Eddie Espinosa who carried the mail on horseback, retrieve the body. He strapped the dead man, by name George Porter, over the saddle of one of his horses and brought him to town where I conducted the inquisition for Sierra County.

My father related more coroner cases than the rest of us, and I can recall some of them that occurred when I was a boy. The usual procedure was to impanel a coroner's jury, then the inquest and autopsy was held, usually in either the old social club hall across the street from the old Mayo saloon, or in the dance hall part of the IOOF hall, the site of the present Masonic Temple.

I recall one held in the latter at a time when one Samuel J. Fraser was the Justice of the Peace. He picked the jury, and most of them were stable men of old who relied on the bottle as a necessary stimulant at a time of need, the judge himself being of the same nature as well as the doctor, Dr. Frederick K. Lord, who incidentally was my uncle.

The only one of the jury I can remember is Old Man Deal, and he had on a long, dark overcoat. The time of year was in the winter when it was raining very hard. The deceased was a man who had died in a lone cabin by the river. They stretched him out on a board, and before they could start with the incision, everyone had to have a drink. Then the operation began.

The doctor made the incision – pretty bad – and that called for another drink. The procedure continued, things got more complicated, another drink was necessary. By this time they were into it, and Old Man Deal got his hands all over blood, which he wiped on his long-tail overcoat, and so on went the autopsy. In due time, it was concluded, and so was the quart of whiskey. I never did hear, or I do not remember, what the man died of, but the case went down in the annals of the local Justice Court, and I assure you it was done in proper course and order.

Dan L. Sharp

Another case my father had when he filled the office was that of a man who also died down on the Middle Yuba River. He had been dead a week in the hot summertime, so you can imagine what kind of case that was. My father impaneled the jury. I do not remember all of them, but one was Charley King, a young man who worked for the local butcher. Another was my cousin Dan Sharp, manager of the S.G. Dry Goods Company in Marysville who was here on vacation. Dr. Lord was again the doctor in charge, and at the outset he had had too much to drink. The operation started.

Dan Sharp couldn't take it, and every few minutes had to run to the door and heave. Charley King pulled up a chair to the table, cocked his feet on it, chewed tobacco, spit every few moments, and took in the whole performance, which did not jar him a bit. Guess he had worked around the local slaughter house too long to be annoyed by anything like this.

Finally, Dr. Lord cut his hand. and realizing what this meant while performing an operation on a body that had been dead that long. he held up all proceedings until he could rush to his home where he had his office and take care of the cut. In a short time he returned, the wound properly taken care of, and also the doctor. The fright of the thing or whatever it was or whatever he took in his office, when he returned he was cold sober and finished the job.

One of the old characteristic Justices of the Peace was Edward Houghtailing. He was a fine old man, but not very particular about his personal habits or about his household. He had a heart of gold and was a very hospitable man. Before he came to town to reside he lived over near Slate Range, and when my father ran the store delivery team, Ed had always asked him in to have lunch - in those days called "dinner"- when he drove the wagon in that neighborhood. Knowing how unsightly his house was, my father always put him off, but finally there came a time when this could not continue. The season was summer, gardens were in, Ed picked the corn, and they had a corn feed, this not being too bad and satisfying the old man's hospitality.

Later he moved to town and had his home and office in a little cabin down back of the hotel in or near what was once China Town. One time, when the Forest Service first came into existence, one of his best friends, Jeff Ritchie, was arrested for starting a fire. Jeff had acquired a habit, thinking that it was too much work to cut wood into small pieces, so he used to put a whole long limb in the stove, leaving it to protrude out into the room, and then shove it in further as it burned.

On this particular day, he became occupied with something and did not notice the fire. The Forest Service had him arrested for setting the fire. He was Ed's very best friend, so to punish him would be painful. Ed found him guilty, fined him $25.00, then paid the fine himself so everything was alright.

Another of Ed's best friends was Frank Parlin, and Ed, as in the case of my father, wanted him to eat with him. Frank put it off as long as he could, but finally had to accept and forebear. He thought the safest thing would be fried eggs, so he told Ed he would enjoy that sort of supper.

They went to Ed's cabin, and Ed steamed up a good hot fire in the stove, put the frying pan on, and was about to fry the eggs. He kept a bottle of olive oil behind the stove for such purpose, and just before putting the oil in the pan, he remarked to Frank that before he started he would have to draw his water and so he produced a catheter, ran it down into the bottle of olive oil, stepped out, drew his water, came back in, poured the oil out of the bottle into the pan, and cooked Frank's eggs, which you can imagine, were very appetizing.

The last Justice of the Peace of Slate Range Township before the county consolidated all townships into one was Samuel J. Fraser. He was a stern man with many good qualities, and also had some that were not so admirable. His worst characteristic was a damnable temper. He hated the Catholics and made no bones of it, and many other people he did not like. He hated the Labadies when they ran the hotel, and in coming from his home to his office, he had to walk past the front of the hotel. Sometimes the guests would leave one of the chairs on the front walkway, and whenever he came by and there was a chair in the way, he would pick it up and fling it out into the middle of the street.

Whenever he did not like someone, he stopped speaking to them. He did not speak to my father for many years. When I was 23 years old, he got mad at me, and in the same manner, quit speaking to me. I refuse to live in a little town and not be on speaking terms with the others, so one day I went over to his place, found him in the chicken yard and had it out with him. He "had heard," as was the usual expression, something that I had said or done about him, all of which was untrue, and so we leveled things off and were the best of friends the rest of his life. Along with the judgeship and notary business he had, he was a barber, and he cut my hair free of charge. When the poor man finally passed away I arranged for his funeral.

CORONER CASES

Another interesting coroner case was that of the suicide of Stanley Lazovski which happened during the Second World War. He was a Russian who was working in the lumber industry. He had no known relatives, and he lived in a small trailer house near Oak Valley, about four miles north of town adjacent to the highway, He had a struggle to get enough desirable food on account of ration stamps.

Apparently, for reasons unknown to anyone, he was unhappy and despondent, so one day he decided to end it all by hanging himself. He took a good sized rope, fastened it around his neck, tied the other end to the lower limb of a small tree, then stood on a chair and jumped off. He could be seen from the highway where it looked as though he were standing there, and several of the local people went up and down the highway while he was hanging there and waved to him. Finally some of the Oak Valley people thought it peculiar so ventured in to see him and were shocked at his having been dangling from said tree for days.

They immediately notified me, and I, in turn, sent for Jerry Sullivan, the then Coroner of Yuba County. Jerry arrived about dusk - it having been late in the afternoon when the discovery was made - and we proceeded over to recover the body, When we cut him down from the tree, his feet were practically touching the ground, but the hanging was successful as far as he was concerned. Everything about his trailer and camp was intact, all his possessions and money on his person had been untouched. There was no indication of any foul play or robbery, etc.

Another local Russian resident, Nick Rothe, in commenting on the act. remarked, "Val, I don't see why Stanley did it. He wasn't married," The body was brought back here, and I conducted his funeral, burying him in the local cemetery, Then, after the funeral was over, all of his possessions had to be taken care of. Having no relatives, it came under the jurisdiction of the public administrators. There was apparently little value to his belongings, but the county had been out the expense in the case, so I told the PA that if he approved, I would have all of his stuff brought into town, and at an appointed time I would hold a public auction and dispose of it. A fitting date was set and advertised, and at the appointed time, people came from far and near, and our store was crowded. I started off in the regular fashion of an auctioneer, and before the afternoon was over, sold every single item that he owned, from the old Ford car down to his old Pocket Ben watch which cost a dollar to him and would not even run, but I sold it for $1.50. Over $300 was obtained for the county, which covered the expense in the case and took care of the disposition of all the odds and ends left by the man.

This happened shortly after my wife and I were married, and she had quite a ball out of it, heckling me after every sale by calling out "Sold American," it being a radio advertisement for Lucky Strike cigarettes at the time.

A MURDER CASE

One murder case created considerable interest. On a chilly night we had retired and about 11:30 the door bell sounded, and a young married couple appeared advising me that a man had been murdered. Not wanting to send for the sheriff or coroner before I knew the facts and if it were true, the wife and I immediately dressed and proceeded up the pavement to the highway, where, sure enough, about two miles away, in a parked car, were three people: a man, his wife, and her brother, the latter having been murdered with bullet holes in his neck and back, and the survivors being in an intoxicated condition, The door of the car was open, and the dead man about ready to slide out into the highway, so we pushed him back in the car and shut the door.

I had phoned Constable Marquardt before we left town, so he soon arrived at the scene, and we came back to town to telephone the sheriff, The survivors gave us a yarn that some passerby had come along, and in an attempted robbery had slain the brother, but the final analysis was that the two men became enraged in a quarrel, and the brother shot him and pleaded guilty and was sentenced to prison on a manslaughter charge,.

We spent almost the entire night out there in the cold, as it took time for the officers to get here from Marysville, When they finally arrived, the photographer had forgotten the flash bulbs, so we had to continue to wait until he went back to Grass Valley, awakened a druggist, and got some bulbs. Finally the coroner claimed the dead man, the sheriff the other two, and then had the car brought to town.

A MYSTERY

A man by the name of Stewart came to the county and took up

his residence at the old PG&E mill in Slate Range. He had been here some little time, was a miserly sort of character and not very well-liked, being a braggart and gloating over what he called a valuable collection of old and rare coins.

On Washington's birthday, with considerable snow on the ground, a couple from Grass Valley came up, went over there, and were in search of a Christmas tree. They happened to see tracks in the snow leading to an old abandoned mining shaft, followed them, and there in the bottom of said shaft, which was some 30 feet deep, saw the body of a man, which was Stewart's. The house showed signs of foul play, with an old hatchet and considerable blood strewn about the place.

They gave the alarm, and in due time, Sheriff Charley McCoy arrived, and the body was recovered, the man having been chopped with the hatchet and also shot with a pistol. The whole thing was a mystery, but after a few days, a man from Grass Valley reported to the sheriff that his kid brother and another boy had been up here on a motorcycle, and he suspected that they committed the crime. The boys were taken into custody, their trip here verified, and they confessed, robbery being the motive, and they were sent to prison.

Sheriff McCoy, who was one of the best politicians in the country, made a big thing out of it, but the mystery never would have been solved had not the brother told him about it. The sheriff would not bring the boys back to Camptonville for a preliminary hearing because he stated that he feared they would be lynched. This was a lot of baloney because the victim was scarcely known here, and not liked by anyone, and besides, I don't believe that the local people would lynch anyone. They are not the type of people to do such things, The story of this was written up in detective magazines, highly colored and flavored as usual, and not authentic.

One amusing instance in the case was the fact that the dead man had some mail in the post office, and the sheriff thought that it might contain some clues to the identity of the murderers, so he demanded Postmaster Lydia Groves give it to him. She refused to do it.

He got mad as a wet hen and asked me to force her to do so. I informed him that she was doing what she was supposed to and should not give it to him, and finally he got the Post Office Department in San Francisco to tell her to give it to him. After he got it, there was nothing of any value in it whatever.

WEDDINGS

In the pioneer days, the local judges officiated at many weddings, but as soon as the three-day law relative to the license came in. their business subsided in that respect. Also in those days, a judge could not go out of his township to officiate, nor could a license from another county be used. When Joseph Nuttall went to get married, they obtained the license in Nevada City and expected to get married here. it could not be done, so another license had to be obtained in Marysville. After it was all over, Joe took the Nevada City license back to the County Clerk in Nevada City for a refund, but the clerk refused to give it to him.

The first wedding I performed took place in the old IOOF Hall and was a big public affair and the first wedding to take place locally. The bride was a member of the high school graduating class, and the groom was a young man sniping on the river. The community joined in making it a big affair. The date was set as the same day of the local high school graduation and an orchestra from the Marysville High School came up to provide the necessary music.

The local people furnished the gown, the cake and other incidentals, and everything went off in regular order. About 500 people attended. First the graduation exercises, then the ceremony, and then the crowd danced the rest of the night. The old dance hall floor had some slivers in it, and the bride's gown caught a couple of times, but no one knew it (except the bride). My next wedding ceremony took place at Strawberry Valley in the school house where a similar wedding took place. excepting there was no graduation in conjunction with it. When I drove up in front of the school house, a couple of long-whiskered natives remarked, "There's the preacher now."

I could not stay after the ceremony, but was told later that this affair lasted until seven o'clock the next morning and that some of the participants brought wine by the bucketful, so there would be no reason to end the festivities too soon!

Weddings increased locally after the three-day license law was repealed, and I still have one now and then. I have preformed ceremonies also in Grass Valley and one in Lake County at which Governor Knight of California was best man. Although I gladly officiate, I am not always cheerful about wedding ceremonies. They always seem somewhat sad or make me sad, and sometimes my voice "cracks" a little, whereas I have never faltered at a funeral service.

In my thirty years in office I have never yet made a charge or received anything for either a wedding or a funeral. The poor guy at the wedding is in for enough trouble without my making him pay for it!

CONSTABULARY

We cannot refer to the judiciary without mentioning the constabulary or the Constable's Office. And in this, I regret that I didn't record more of the activities of that guardian of the law because there have been many interesting incidents.

The most colorful constable I knew was I.D. Bray, his full name being Iredell Donaldson Bray He is the one I referred to in a previous chapter relative to embarrassment in church. He was a very fastidious man and neat as could be. He had a white Van Dyke beard, wore light blue or green check gingham jumpers (for a shirt, starched trousers, and cowboy boots with the pants leg in one boot and out of the other. He limped and walked with a cane. In summer he wore a straw hat.

He lived in a neat cabin to the left of the highway as you come into town at the lower entrance. When he was ill before his death, he asked one of his male nurses to look in the bottom of the wood box wherein he found $1,500 in $20.gold pieces, his safe place for keeping it.

I.D. Bray commanded the law here for many years and was stern and fair in his administering it. Around 1911, the game warden had arrested a man for blasting fish in Oregon Creek and Constable I.D. Bray incarcerated him in the local jail, which, of course, had no bathroom or cooking facilities. Thus the Constable had to take the prisoner to the hotel for his meals. On this particular day he took him there for lunch (dinner at noon in that day and age), and while starting to eat in the dining room, he told the Custodian of the Law that he had to go to the toilet. So, Iredell, a trusting soul, even with desperados, permitted the man to head towards the bathroom unattended. I, at this moment an inquisitive kid of 11 years who always saw about everything that ever went on, saw this man rush out of the parlor door, jump over the porch railing, and go like a deer towards old China Town. Had I given the alarm, he would have been captured at once, but I was too scared to say anything, fearing that the man might take vengeance out later, so kept quiet about it.

After a moderate time, when he did not come back, Bray became suspicious and upon looking in the lavatory, finding the culprit absent, gave the general alarm, and everyone in the dining room, as well as those in the store and saloon, took up the chase for the fugitive. The fellow ran down to the bedrock, and soon the posse was catching up with him.. He rounded a curve and ditched himself quickly in a ditch. One of the teamsters for the store saw him, but made believe otherwise. Apparently he did not want to tackle him.

He kept running, but the next man in pursuit, one of the clerks in the store, nailed the prisoner, and the rest of the posse caught up, and he was taken back to captivity and firmly locked back in the jail house without being permitted to finish his dinner. Constable Bray disappeared and shortly returned with an old bread pan full of ashes, unlocking the door, and put it inside the jail, informing the culprit that from now on, that was his toilet. The man was tried in the local court, found guilty, and sentenced to the Yuba County jail.

CHAPTER 12

DISASTERS

THE FIRE OF 1908

The worst disaster which befell every and all of our old pioneer towns was fire. Since the advent of the Forest Service, from propaganda spread by the radio, press, etc., all danger is focused on the forest fire danger.

This is a lot of nonsense. It is to be admitted, however, that during the past 50-some-odd years of the Forest Service regime, there is an imminent danger from the forest due to the immense accumulation of junk, trash, and rubbish which has in all these years been multiplying in our forests. However, in all my life I have known of only one forest fire in our mountains which destroyed every building, that being in 1959. When in the big Camptonville fire, a couple of buildings in Pike City burned, and even these could have been saved if they had been properly back-fired.

All of the fires I have ever known internally in the towns or in the buildings burned, the first big fire destroying Camptonville was in 1889 in which the major part of the town was consumed. The town was, of course, built back, and now and then, someone's house would be lost, and the next big fire took place in March 1908.

This took place on a March day when a terrific north wind was blowing, there were no men in town, all out working, and of course, the water supply was inadequate. Someone in the post office took occasion to burn a quantity of waste paper in the stove.

A burning piece got on the shake roof, and within a short time, a raging fire ensued. In the course of a few hours. It burned the Express office, store, saloon (and the Masonic Hall over it), two stage barns, blacksmith shop, butcher shop, social dance hall, livery barn and, outbuildings and dwellings, with nothing being saved, a ruined, smoldering mass remaining.

The only thing standing in the entire business section of town was a soap-stone vault in my grandfather's office in which he had presence of mind enough to carry the store cash register (which ordinarily would require two people to lift) therein and lock the door.

As soon as the situation cooled enough to do anything, my grandfather obtained a flag pole, a large American flag, which he had placed in said vault, and had his picture taken with waving hat in hand on top of the vault and composed a verse.

He later had cards made for his friends with the picture thereon, the verse on the back of it. Instead of printing his name completely, he had a picture of a billy goat, a charging bull, and his last name, it representing, of course, his name: William Bull Meek. On the sides of the goat and the bull he had emblems of the Masonic Fraternity, the Shriners, and the Elks, to which orders he belonged. The Elks took exception to this, considering it advertising (which it was not, the cards being made for good fellowship only, and after a hassle about it, he became disgusted and withdrew from the order.

He immediately started to clean up the ruins and rebuild. It was an awful mess. One thing alone I can recall: enough baked potatoes to feed an army where the potato stock was stored in a cellar. His aim was to build back a "fire-proof" town (practically an impossibility). He did, however, do the nearest to it he could. Along with trying to make the buildings fire-proof, he saw to it that there was space for a vacant lot between each of the buildings.

Thus, like the phoenix, another town arose from the ruins. The two main buildings, the store and saloon, both two-story, high-ceiling structures, were made of concrete very heavily constructed. This was before the days of automobiles or machinery. All the rock, gravel and cement had to be hauled by horse team, and all shoveling and cement mixing by hand and the sweat of the brow. There were no cement mixers. It was all mixed by two notorious men: Dutch Jake and an Irishman.

It was all carried up to the forms on inclined planks via wheelbarrows. At the time this was going on, the Nevada City Narrow Gauge Railroad was building a new trestle (a cut-off) over Bear River. John Flint Kidder, the president of the railroad, and my grandfather were very good friends, so he gave my grandfather all the railroad rails from the old track and trestle, and they were hauled to Camptonville by horse team and were linked together every few feet all around the inside walls of the two cement buildings, providing extra strength to the construction.

During the period of reconstruction, a make-shift town had been set up, with a temporary P.O., store, and most importantly, a saloon. A bunk house had to be erected to house some of the workers on the building. In front of the temporary saloon, which was located on China Lane, W.B. erected a sign: "Wet house for dry people" and over the door to the bunk house he placed the sign "Dry house for wet people."

All the lumber for the building was cut and milled by the Slate Range Mill seven miles NW of town, which at one time was owned and operated by W.B. All of the interiors were made of the finest sugar pine lumber. Of course, all labor was by the day's pay and it is needless to say that in those days, the same as in these, there were a few "gold brickers" on the job.

This could be evidenced later when remodeling was done in the store by observance of an interesting number of nails having been used on shelving, there being a nail almost every inch or two thus taking more time to build, making the job last longer.

The world over, from the dark ages to the Space Age, there has been ever prevalent, the fallacy of some human brains - the act of "killing the goose that laid the golden egg." W.B. had his foreman in the construction a man named Stewart. I was too young to comprehend, but I had many times heard it said later that this fellow Stewart "took" W. B. in the erection of these buildings.

By late summer the buildings were completed, and the date of September 9, 1908, was set for the dedication and opening, and a general celebration was in order, and as usual procedure at the expense of Bill Meek.

For this festive occasion, the town was bedecked in red, white and blue bunting and flags. The second story of the store building was made into a huge dancehall with a stage for the orchestra or band. At the end of China Lane on the outskirts of China Town a framework was set up covered with large tree limbs to create shade, tables erected, a large iron kettle set up , and Pete Mondada, a life-long friend of the family and an excellent cook specializing in Italian-Swiss cookery, was at hand, and for a couple of days, served his spaghetti and chicken to all participants in the celebration (at the expense of Bill Meek), which concession, you may well be aware, was highly "patronized."

A big all-night dance took place on the 9th. A bootblack stand (something of unheard of and foreign to Camptonville) was set up on the store porch. It goes without saying that whiskey flowed freely during these few days, and naturally the entire dedication of the new modern town was a huge success.

Although I do not wish to criticize my grandfather, because under the same conditions I probably would have done the same thing, but he did make a huge mistake in building such large expensive buildings when smaller and more conservative and condensed would have not only been as good but better, all of which caused him to go into bankruptcy a short time later in 1911.

BRANDY CITY EXPLOSION

Mining was what started the community. It was the principal industry and livelihood for years. With it was much anticipation, anxiety, success, failure, heartbreak, and catastrophe. About the worst of the latter in my time or to my knowledge was the Brandy City explosion in the early winter of 1915.

Brandy City was a lively hydraulic mining camp nine miles north by trail and about 18 miles by wagon road. It was operated by Jewish people from San Francisco. It was a typical hydraulic mining camp. It had a boarding house, a saloon, a post office, and several dwellings. It was a rugged place in winter, snow attaining deep proportions. Mail was carried there three days a week by three pack trains from Camptonville coming over the trail, which went out through Oak Valley, crossing the North Yuba River through a covered bridge near where Cherokee Creek runs into the river.

For several months that fall they were busy running a tunnel drift into a heavy and solid granite bank to be blasted down so that it could be worked. When the drift was completed, it was filled with an entire railroad carload of dynamite hauled from Nevada City by horse team. This was to be one of the biggest charges of dynamite ever to be set off in these parts. When it was ready to be exploded, all the miners gathered in and near a blacksmith shop where the fuse was to be ignited.

Instead of the dynamite exploding as it should have done, it ignited and burned, and a huge cloud of poisonous gas bellowed forth, and with a north wind behind it, hovered over the hydraulic mine pit, settling over the miners assembled there to witness the explosion.

They saw it coming and started to run to safety Some of them reached a safe distance, but the majority were trapped and fell to the ground overcome with the poisonous air. As a result, four apparently died at once, and a score of others was overcome, some taking months to recover. The dead were Ernest Godfrey, Tom Sadler, Joe Tioni, and Jack Hays.

An alarm was telephoned to Camptonville, and Dr. Lord, accompanied by volunteer workers, immediately set out for Brandy City, and Dr. Muller of Nevada City was sent to the distressed area.

Christmas Day, December 25, 1915, was a sad day in Camptonville. The bodies were brought to town by horse and wagon, and a funeral for the four was conducted from the IOOF Hall with internment in the local cemetery. Dr. Lord, who was a sentimental man with a kind heart, cried like a baby.

TRAGEDY AT SNOWDEN HILL

Snowden Hill was another old mine of the drift grade type characterized by huge rocks and boulders. It came down from pioneer days, with some interesting incidents. After many years of operation by the various owners or lessors, it became a pretty rundown concern and was leased by Andy and Jack Wolff who ran it themselves for quite some time.

Andrew and Jack Wolff. in dark shirts, Snowden Hill Mine

Many human beings work or are in an environment of danger, but have been in it for so long they have no fear of what might or could happen. The tunnel in this mine had become in a dangerous condition, the timbers being so rotten that one could poke a finger through them. A visitor would be afraid to enter, but not the brothers who scoffed at any danger.

One day as they were working a huge cave, when material came plunging down from the overhead cavern with tons of rocks and boulders thundering down from said cavern and caught Jack Wolff, pinning him to the floor of the tunnel in such a manner that he could not get out. Still being conscious although badly hurt. his brother Andy telephoned for help, and a number of men from

Camptonville rushed to the mine and struggled frantically to remove the tons of rock on top of him.

When this happened, the state had a convict camp at Depot Hill constructing Highway 49, and one prisoner in particular was strong as a bull. He was sent up, and to the amazement of many, brought out rocks that four men could not lift. After a couple of days' struggle, poor Jack was freed, but the injury and shock were too much for him. He died on route to Nevada City.

Here ends the manuscript of Acton Cleveland's memoirs. I suspect he planned to get back to them some day and include some finishing touches, or maybe there are more pages yet to be found. This is what survived to date.

- Editor

APPENDIX I

JUDGE ACTON CLEVELAND TO RETIRE; COURT TO CLOSE

A colorful chapter of Yuba County history will come to an end tomorrow. when Judge Acton M. Cleveland retires and his Camptonville District Court is abolished. A 53-year county employee, Cleveland has been in charge of Camptonville judicial matters since 1933 when he was appointed justice of the peace. That title was changed to District Court Judge by the state in 1949.

His service to the county started back in 1923. when he was appointed as deputy county assessor. He views his forced retirement from the bench with mixed emotions. While consolidation with the Marysville District Court was inevitable, he said, it represents a continuing trend of the state taking the mechanics of justice away from the people. Even if his district had not been abolished by the county supervisors, Cleveland would have to resign tomorrow because he is not an attorney judge. Healthy and alert at 76 years. Cleveland said he would stay on the bench if it weren't for these new regulations.

Reflecting on his long judicial career, Cleveland said justice in the Yuba hills region was always practiced a little differently than in the flatlands of Marysville. His system didn't have 'a lot of high-toned performances, but it did the job," he said. "More cases never got on books than those did." he said because he saw his duty as peacemaker and "father confessor" as well as presiding over court.

During his tenure, it wasn't uncommon for the judge to be awakened at 2 a.m. by a complainant who wanted justice done to the assailant who had punched him in the nose. The judge said that in such cases he wouldn't usually do anything until the next morning, when tempers often had cooled to the point where any notion of filing charges had been forgotten.

But as Justice of the Peace, there were times when he would be called out of bed for other, more important reasons.

"I remember about 25 years ago, a girl knocked on my door about 11 p.rn. and said that a man had been murdered about three miles up the road," the judge recalled. "Sure enough, there was a guy half in, half out of his car with a bullet hole in his neck." Since he was a deputy coroner in those days – one of the many duties of a Justice of the Peace - he had to call the district attorney and sheriff, who arrested a suspect on the scene. "We didn't get done with that mess until four in the morning," Cleveland said. "We were supposed to be everything for the people in those days. When someone got in trouble, they got the Justice of the Peace. It didn't matter what the hour was. "That was what they expected," he said. "Each district elected a man to fill the void. If he didn't do the job, they'd kick him out," Cleveland said. "Now it's not like it used to be and not like it should be."

Serving as the judicial arm of the government is a tradition in the judge's family, dating back to his grandfather. In the years following the turn of the century, Yuba County was divided into seven townships. with each having its own judge.

Earl Cleveland, the judge's father, served as judge in the Slate Range Township Court for many years until county supervisors did away with the system and consolidated all courts into one district with one judge and constable. The one-court system lasted until 1928, when supervisors, no doubt tired of hearing complaints from Camptonville residents, created three districts — Camptonville. Marysville, and Wheatland. Each was to have its own judge. "The trouble was nobody wanted to be judge," Cleveland recalled. "Finally, I talked my grandfather, William Bull Meek, into it, but only on the condition that 1 did all the work. That was the understanding." Meek stepped down in May of 1933 because "it was making him nervous," and Cleveland was appointed to take over. His title changed from Justice of the Peace to Judge in 1949.

During those years, his monthly salary rose from S20 to $500, although his case load never changed much. In addition to being judge, Cleveland also represented that portion of the county in road matters for 40 years and was also deputy tax assessor until about ten years ago. The population of his district has always stayed at about 500 because "There isn't any room for more." While his duties haven't changed much over the years, Cleveland said the laws he swore to uphold have, and usually not for the better. "l don't think well of the changes," he said bluntly. "They're taking the jurisdiction away from the people. We had the informality in those days that you don't have now. You didn't need an attorney."

Cleveland didn't have very many jury trials in his court (he could recall only three) because "back in the good old days" if a person was found guilty, he'd have to pay not only the fine, but a justice fee and sometimes a constable fee as well. He said the current "fuss" over conditions at the Yuba County Jail is another example of changes he does not approve of.

Conditions at the jail now "are a lot better than some of (the prisoners) have at home," the judge said. Jails, he said, are supposed to be places where people do not want to be. "And what about rights?" he asked. They [the petitioners] have rights, but the rest of us don't have any. We can't protect ourselves or our property against these people. Our government ls failing somewhere when these conditions exist." ln his day, Cleveland said, a man who shot and killed another man would be hung, period. "And if he was crazy, then all the more reason to hang him."

The judge has remained extremely active in judicial and other public activities. He's a past president of the Judges, Marshals and Constables Association of California and served as convention chairman of the group for 19 years. He's been the Camptonville correspondent for *The Appeal-Democrat* since 1924. The judge has served in Yuba City, Biggs, Gridley, Grass Valley, Nevada City and Downieville courts when called. In fact, he ended his long career with yesterday's visit to the Sierra County Justice Court in Downieville, where he presided at several preliminary hearings.

Cleveland recently moved from his lifelong home in Camptonville to Yuba City, mainly because he got "sick and tired of the snow and ice." Besides, he said, most of his old friends in Camptonville have either died or moved away. "l can walk down Plumas Street and meet more people that I know," he said. He will remain active in Camptonville, where he owns property and still serves as secretary to the Gravel Range Masonic Lodge there and secretary to the Camptonville Cemetery District.

And he will probably go on marrying and burying people when called, services for which he has never charged a penny.

"It's been a pleasurable chore," the judge said of his legal career. "I've been able to help out a lot of people and perhaps have fulfilled some of the reasons I was put on earth."

(Source: Dyer, Steve. "Judge Acton Cleveland To Retire; Court To Close," Judges, Marshals and Constables Magazine, Judges, Marshalls, and Constables Association, Vol 32, No. 1, March 1977, pp. 1-3,

---

THE GOOD JUDGE ACTON CLEVELAND

By Bonnie Wayne McGuire

When you visit the little Sierra town of Camptonville, California you'll see a main street named Cleveland Avenue. Whenever I see it I'm reminded of an experience Mel had when we were in the trucking business. He was hauling logs in the area when a highway patrolman weigh-master pulled him over to weigh the load. The truck was in a bad position and the officer seemed to be having trouble.

His scales said the truck was over-weight, so he wrote out a ticket. Then he weighed it again, when the truck was in the normal position. His scales revealed the load was legal. Mel asked him to nullify the ticket, but he refused, jumped in his vehicle and headed for Sacramento. When Mel got to a phone, he called the Nevada County District Attorney to see if they would stop him. The DA refused...adding that "Mel was on the other side of the fence."

Eventually, Camptonville's Judge Acton Cleveland heard about it and was very nice. He told Mel that if he ever had any trouble in the future to call him and he'd come down to mediate. The fine was a hefty $700, so we wrote to Governor Edmund Brown to see if he'd investigate the problem. We never heard anything from him, and paid the fine. Later another highway patrolman kept harassing Mel when he was on the road. He'd pull him over and try to find something wrong. Finally Mel blew up and asked him what was going on. He replied, "You tried to get my buddy's job."

Typical of human nature to always blame someone else for consequences when we make bad choices. With the passage of time what goes around comes around. Evidently, Mel wasn't the only victim of the wayward officer who cost us so much grief and money. The officer was eventually barred from the area.

Acton Cleveland was the grandson of William Bull Meek and his family were long-time residents of Camptonville. Just after the turn of the century, Yuba County was divided into seven townships. Each township had its own judge, and Earl Cleveland, Acton's father, served as the judge in the Slate Range Township Court for years until the county supervisors consolidated all the courts into one district with one judge and constable. This one-court system operated until 1928 when supervisors, in response to complaints from Camptonville residents, created three districts (Camptonville, Marysville, Wheatland). Each was to have its own judge.

"The trouble was that nobody wanted to be judge," Cleveland recalled in an article in Judges', Marshals' and Constables' Magazine, the official monthly publication of the Judges', Marshals' and Constables' Association, in March of 1977. "Finally I talked my grandfather, William Bull Meek, into it, but only on the condition that I did all the work. That was the understanding."

According to Cleveland, Meek stepped down in May 1933 because "it was making him nervous," and Acton was appointed to take over the office. Acton Cleveland also represented the Camptonville area in road matters for 40 years and was Deputy Tax Assessor into the 1960s.

Acton worked for Yuba County for 53 years. He was first appointed Deputy County Assessor in 1923 and Justice of the Peace in 1933. In 1949, this title was changed to District Court Judge. In 1977, Acton was forced into retirement as a result of the consolidation of his district with the Marysville District Court and because he was not an attorney judge. In the 1960s Acton Cleveland began to write down his memories.

APPENDIX II

PEOPLE AND PLACES

An Alphabetical List

Dr J. H. Barr and daughter Barbara

BARR, DR. JAMES HOLMES

Dr. James Holmes Barr was born in Scotland on June 22, 1858 and immigrated to the US in 1871. In 1910 he and his family were living at 115 1/2 D Street in Marysville. By 1920, he, his wife, and their son and daughter had moved to 125 6th Street and in 1930 had moved to 126 2nd Street in Yuba City. According to the 1930 US Federal Census, Dr. Barr's home was valued at $15,000, and he owned a radio set. His wife Hedwick T. (Ebert) Barr was born in California on February 4, 1878. Her parents were both German. Dr. Barr worked from his own physician's office during his career in Yuba and Sutter Counties. In 1930, the Barrs had a nephew, Francis Ebert aged seven, living in their household. In 1940, Hedwick Barr's widowed brother James who had also been born in California joined the household. Dr. Barr died in Sutter County on September 9,1940 and is buried in Sutter Cemetery. Hedwick Barr died in Sutter County on December 4, 1966, and is also buried in Sutter Cemetery. *(Sources: US Federal Censuses; FindAGrave.com).*

BILLY WARD'S SALOON

This is most likely the saloon called The Grotto that operated at 222 D Street in Marysville. It was owned by William W. Ward. Ward was originally the owner of the Railroad House saloon at an old railway depot at A and 6th Streets. In 1880, Ward partnered with J.L Murphy in another saloon on D Street, which was possibly The Grotto. Ward was sole owner of The Grotto by 1882, and in 1907 went into partnership with Zan Frye to run The Grotto. The partnership lasted until 1914 when Frye bought him out. The Grotto closed for good in 1918 at the beginning of Prohibition. Company name timeline: W Ward (1882-1907), Ward & Frye (1907-1914), Zan Frye (1914-1918) *(Source: Database of pre-Prohibition liquor distributors and establishments at http://www.pre-pro.com/index.htm)*

BLISS, CHARLES

Charles W Bliss was born about 1825 in New York. He was 38 on July 1, 1863, single, and living in Slate Range, according to his US Civil War Draft Registration Record. *(Source: U.S., Civil War Draft Registrations Records, 1863-1865)*

BLISS, CHESTER ABIEL

Chester A Bliss was born in New York sometime between 1828 and 1834. He died in 1906. According to the United States Civil War Draft Registrations Records, he stated his age as 30 as of July 1, 1863, his marital status as single, and his residence as Slate Range, California. In 1870, he was still making his home in Slate Range in Yuba County and was working as a miner. He enlisted in the National Guard in California on September 8, 1875, and was a corporal. In 1990, *(Sources: California Military Registers 1858-1923; US Federal Census; U.S., Civil War Draft Registrations Records, 1863-1865)*

BLISS, RICHARD H. "DICK"

Richard H. Bliss was born in New York in March 1827, He married Elizabeth Bliss in 1872, and by 1900 they had been married for 28 years. Their daughter Mary E. Bliss, 24, was living with them. His father was from Connecticut, and his mother was from New York. *(Source: US Federal Census)*

BRANDY CITY BURN

Contemporary newspaper accounts of the Brandy City mine disaster.

FOUR MEN DEAD IN DISASTER IN MINE
Powder Half Blasted Burns Causing Deadly Fumes To Overcome Men

BRANDY CITY, Cal.. Dec. 23. — Four men were asphyxiated by powder fumes, three others are unconscious and expected to die, and another is in a serious condition as the result of the failure of a 22,000-pound blast of low-grade powder, set in the Brandy City mine near here, to explode fully. Superintendent G. W. Taylor is the only one with a chance for recovery. In Brandy City, a mile away, the gas fumes were so thick that many persons were affected. No serious injuries, however, were reported. When all was ready, Taylor and the seven miners took refuge in a deep hydraulic cut, some distance away. Others of the crew of about 25 scattered to other places. The blast was set off, but only about one halt of it exploded. The remainder burned, creating a deadly poisonous gas. The draft sent it through the cut in which the eight men had taken refuge, and so dense was it that an hour passed before the rescue could be made. When the men were brought out, E. Godfrey, Jack Hayes and Thomas Sadler were dead, and the other five unconscious. First aid plans, such as miners know, were used to resuscitate the men, but their crude efforts were unavailing. Hurry calls were sent to the nearest camps for physicians, but before they arrived, Joseph Tioni had died. *(Source: Morning Press, Volume 43, Number 312, 24 December 1915)*

FOUR ASPHYXIATED BY POWDER FUMES

ONLY PART OF GREAT BLAST SET IN SIERRA MINE EXPLODES, AND EIGHT MEN ARE TRAPPED BY GAS; FUMES FELT MILE AWAY.

Special to the Union. BRANDY CITY (Sierra Co.),. —Four men were asphyxiated by powder fumes, three others are unconscious and expected to die. and another is in a serious condition as the result of the failure of a 22,000-pound blast of low grade powder set in the Brandy City mine near here to explode fully. The dead are E. Godfrey, .lack Hayes. Thomas Sadler and .Joseph Tioni. Three other miners are expected to die. but Superintendent G. W. Taylor has regained consciousness and has a chance for recovery. In Brandy City a mile away, the gas fumes were so thick that many persons were affected. No serious injuries, however, were reported. The accident is one of the most peculiar in California's long mining history. The tremendous load of powder, said to be the largest amount ever used in a single blast in California mining, was put in 11 holes to tear down 160 feel of the mountainside. Extensive preparations had been made to insure the success of the blast, and when all was ready, Taylor and seven miners took refuge in a deep hydraulic cut some distance away. Others of the crew of about 25 scattered to other places. The blast was set off, but only about one-half of it exploded. The remainder burned, creating a deadly poisonous gas. The draft set through the cut in which the eight men had taken refuge, and so dense was it that an hour passed before the rescue could be made. When the men were brought out, Godfrey. Hayes and Sadler were dead, and the other five unconscious. First aid plans, such as miners know, were used to resuscitate the men, but their crude efforts were unavailing. Hurry calls were sent to the camps for physicians, but when they arrived Joseph Tioni was dying. He passed away early in the evening. The doctors have been able to keep alive the other four, but except for Superintendent Taylor, little hope is held out. Brandy City is a little known mining camp about 30 miles north of Downieville. *(Source: Sacramento Union, Number 54, 24 December 1915)*

BRAY, IRADELL DONALDSON

The one-time constable and snappy dresser of Camptonville was born in 1836. Research indicates he was born in Pulaski, a town in either Tennessee or Kentucky, as both states have one. Bray enlisted in Company C, Kentucky 6th Cavalry Regiment as a private on October 8, 1862, under the command of Colonel Grigsby. According to his application for a military pension filed in 1912, he was taken prisoner at the Battle of Buffington Island (St. George Creek Skirmish), Meigs County, Ohio, in July 1863. This was the largest battle in Ohio during the Civil War and contributed to the capture of Brigadier General John Hunt Morgan, who was trying to escape Union forces across the Ohio River. The Confederates were defeated, and more than half of their 1,700-man force was captured and imprisoned at Rock Island, Illinois. Bray was released on March 1, 1865. In answer to a question on the pension application form "Were you paroled?" Bray answered, "I was not." And his answer to "Did you pledge an oath of allegiance to the United States government?" Bray answered, "I did not." Bray was living in Slate Range by 1867. He died in Camptonville in 1919. P.J. Butz and S.F. Price were signed as witnesses to his will, a handwritten document in which he bequeathed his estate to his nieces and nephews, the children of William Bray of Fredericktown, Missouri. *(Sources: U.S., Civil War Soldier Records and Profiles, 1861-1865; Confederate Kentucky Volunteers War 1861-65;*

Wikipedia, "Battle of Buffington Island; Ancestry.com. California, Wills and Probate Records, 1850-1953)

BYRD, THOMAS JACKSON

Thomas Jackson Byrd was born in Georgia in March 1834. His parents were both from South Carolina. The US Federal Census for 1900 lists his spouse as Rosie B. Byrd and their marriage date as 1887. According to federal census records, he was single miner in 1870 and a widowed farmer with a 14 year old daughter in 1880. In 1910, he was working as a gold miner. In 1920, he was living in Foster Bar. Byrd died in Camptonville in 1932 and is buried in Camptonville Cemetery. He had a daughter Sarah N., who was born in California in 1869 and died in August 1883 at the age of 14. She is buried in Camptonville Cemetery. According to the 1880 US Federal Census, she is listed as a Native American. *(Sources: US Federal Census 1900, 1920)*

CARTASSO, GIACOMO

Giacomo Cartasso was born in Italy about 1876 and arrived in the United States in 1898. According to his California voter registration information 1934-1844, he was a Socialist and a farmer. He was married to Maggiorina Reggiardo Cartasso, who was born in Italy in 1881, and they had two children, Fred J. and Dena. Maggiorina Reggiardo immigrated alone without family members at the age of 22, departing from Genoa, Italy on May 11, 1903, and arriving in New York on May 27, 1903, on the ship *Liguria*. Both husband and wife were naturalized US citizens by 1930. In the 1930 US Federal Census, he is listed as owning a home at 395 Adams Street and managing a clothing store in Alameda, California. According to Cartasso's 1906 voter registration information, he was a merchant living at 707 Broadway in Alameda. He registered for the draft in World War I; his draft card states he is of medium physical build, of medium height, with black hair and grey eyes. His birth date is listed as January 1, 1876, and he was living with his wife at 544 6th Street in Oakland. His 1922 and 1926 voter registrations list his residence as Alameda, his occupation as merchant, and his political party affiliation as Republican. In 1932, he was still living in Alameda, but stated he was retired. By 1934, he had moved to 365 Warwick Street in Alameda and was working as a "superintendent." He declined to state his political party affiliation in 1932 and 1934. He moved to Camptonville sometime between 1934 and 1944 as he is listed in the voter registration logs for those years state he is a farmer and a Democrat. Cartasso died in 1959 in Nevada County. *(Sources: California, Voter Registrations, 1900-1968; US Federal Census 1930; New York, Passenger Lists, 1820-1957; California, Death Index, 1940-1997; U.S., World War I Draft Registration Cards, 1917-1918)*

CLEVELAND, EARL LEROY

Earl Cleveland was born August 5, 1879. His father was Thomas Russel Cleveland who was born in Iowa, and his mother was Martha Jane Moody of Spenceville, California. His father died in an explosion at a powder house in North San Juan, California, in 1883. His mother remarried John S. Langdon of Nevada City, California, in 1894. Earl married Lottie Adeline Meek (1879-1960), the daughter of William Bull Meek and Mary Robbins Meek in 1900 He died on June 7,1961, in Sacramento, California, at the age of 81. *(Sources: US Federal Census)*

CLEVELAND, LOTTIE ADELINE MEEK

Lottie A. Meek Cleveland was born on June 29, 1879,and died April 26,1960. She was the daughter of William Bull Meek and Mary Robbins Meek. In the 1920 US Federal Census she is listed as working as a bookkeeper in a general merchandise store. Living in the Cleveland household in 1920, in addition to herself and her husband Earl, were their son Acton Meek Cleveland, age 19, and John F. Lord, a nephew aged 7. In 1930, the Cleveland's were living in Sacramento with John F. Lord. In 1940, still living in Sacramento, Lottie and Earl Cleveland included in their household Lottie's mother Mary Meek, age 81, and granddaughter Earlyne Meek, age 13. *(Source: US Federal Census)*

COHN, ISAAC "ICHI"

This is most likely Isaac Gaballe Cohn, who was the manager of the J.G. Cohn clothing store, which was owned by his brother Jacob Cohn on the corner of D and 2nd Streets in Marysville in

1904. He was born on January 31,1845 in Budzyn, Wielkopolskie, Poland. He arrived in New York in December1880 and became a naturalized citizen on October 14, 1892.In 1906, the large J.G Cohn store was sold to the S.E. King Company after nearly 50 years in business. The Cohn Company was a pioneer dry goods establishment in Marysville and its largest. The S.E. King Company was in the same line of business and purchased the Cohn store and its building. J.G. Cohn kept the "gentlemen's furnishing goods department," but its business was relocated to the space previously occupied by the King Company. The deal between these two firms was one of the largest to occur in Marysville and was especially notable because the Cohn firm had been so long established in the city. Isaac Cohn died in Yuba County on January 3,1926 in Yuba County. *(Sources: US Federal Census; Sacramento Union, Number 24, 17 March 1906' Sacramento Union, Number 54, 16 April 1906)*

DEAL, JOHN EDWARD

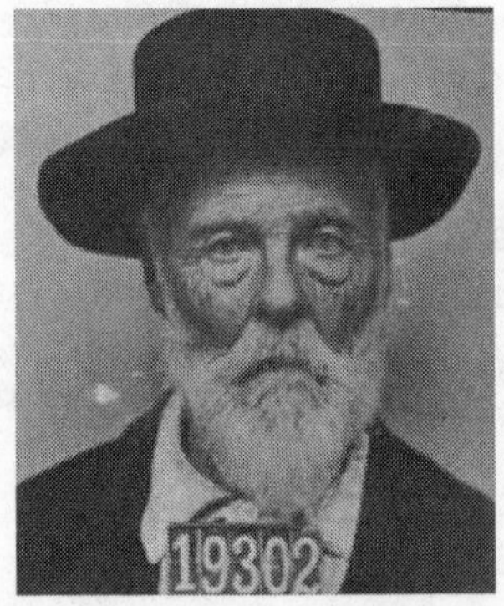

John Edward Deal was born in North Carolina on October 1, 1828. Records indicate he came to California in either 1850 or 1854, In 1860, he and Mary Ann Phillips, who was born in Pennsylvania in 1843, had a son Robert Henry Deal on June 28 at Railroad Hill in Yuba County. John was working as a miner. At some point in 1850 the couple moved to Bridgeport, and in 1862, their son Joseph Asberry Deal (1862–1939) was born in Camptonville. In 1863, John and Mary Ann were married on April 15 in their home in Camptonville, probably by a traveling minister or justice of the peace. They went on to have several more children: John Wesley Deal (1864–1911), Jacob Ellison Deal(1867–1941), Mary Jane Deal((1872–1938), James Edward Deal(1872–1944), Benjamin Howard Deal (1875–1944), Samuel Crawford Deal (1877–1917), Rosa Nell Deal (1879–1892), and Grace Angeline Deal(1882–1923). Mary Ann died in 1899. In 1900, John was listed in the US Federal Census as a miner and a widower. In

1901, he was indicted and convicted of the rape of a 14-year-old girl and sentenced to five years in San Quentin. He was released in 1905. John Edward Deal died on July 31,1913 , at the age of 85 in Camptonville where he was living with his son Jacob at the time of his death. *(Sources: US Federal Census; The Sutter Co. Farmers Newspaper Dec. 13, 1901; Family stories and photos shared at ancestry.com by nolan1928 originally shared this on 15 June 2012).*

DIEDRICK, JACOB "DUTCH JAKE"

Jacob Diedrick was born January 5, 1847, reportedly in Germany, and naturalized on November 19, 1860 in Butte, California. He died on July 1, 1945, in Yuba County and is buried in the Camptonville Cemetery. He was known by Camptonville residents as "Dutch Jake." According to Leland Pauly, "Jake was the biggest storyteller and some of his stories weren't exactly true. He always said he was about ten years older than he really was and he fought Indians all the way from Utah to California. But he was a tough worker and tough drinker. Jake and Pete Butz poured all that cement for the Mayo Building and the store, which was a lot bigger than the Mayo Building. They poured it all by hand. That was after the 1908 fire. I bet Frank Meggers made that marker (in the cemetery). Meggers was a great friend of Jake's. He took him around and took care of him and everything. Meggers gave me Jake's old Put 'n Take game." *(Sources: US Federal Census; The Camptonville Connection, Hank Meals)*

CLAIMS MUSHROOM PICKING TITLE

CAMPTONVILLE. Calif.--(INS)- Jacob Deitrich today claimed the mushroom picking championship of this region. He found a mushroom 18 inches in diameter, weighing five pounds." *(Sources: The Ogden Standard-Examiner from Ogden, Utah · Sunday, May 25, 1930; California, Death Index, 1940-1997; The Camptonville Connection, Hank Meals)*

ESPINOSA, EDDIE

In 1939, Eddie Espinosa, driver of the Pike City Stage, drew national attention when newspapers across the US printed a story praising his "trigger speed" and described how, when he saw a hawk carrying a squirrel in its talons, "whipped out his six-shooter and shot the hawk dead." The story did not mention the condition of the squirrel. *(Source: San Mateo Times, Sep 23, 1939, p. 7)*

FRASER, SAMUEL J.

Samuel J. Fraser was born in Canada in about 1858. His father was from Scotland, and his mother was from Ireland. He immigrated to the US in 1884 and became a naturalized citizen in Yuba County on May 15, 1890. In 1910, Fraser lived with his wife Lizzie on a street named "Camptonville Road" with their children Georgia Fraser, 19; Glynn Fraser, 16; and Norvel Fraser, 6. Elizabeth Fraser was born about 1861 in California, the daughter of Welsh parents. Fraser was working in his own gold mine at the time, but stated on the US Federal Census that he had been out of work for 56 weeks. In 1920, the Fraser household comprised Samuel, his wife, and his youngest son Norval, who was 16. Fraser was still mining gold and owned his own home and mine. He died in San Francisco at the age of 72 on February 13, 1930. *(Sources: US Federal Census; California State Court Naturalization Records, 1850-1986; California Death Index, 1905-1939)*

> JUSTICE OF PEACE RESIGNS
>
> Special to the Union. MARYSVILLE, Yuba Co., July B.—-S. J. Fraser, justice of the peace at Slate Range township, near Camptonville. tendered his resignation to the Yuba board of supervisors today, and the same was accepted. The board did not appoint any one to fill the vacancy. Fraser gave as his reason for resigning that he was working out of Camptonville and could not attend to the duties of the office. *(Source: Sacramento Union, Number 9, 9 July 1919Sacramento Union, Number 118, 26 October 1913)*

GAGE, MOSES DWIGHT

W.B. Meek said Gage was "hired to teach school and did a little preaching on the side," but he had already had an interesting life before arriving in Camptonville. Gage was born January 4, 1829 in New York. In 1860, he was living in Pendleton, Indiana with his wife Mary and their two children, Ella age two and Emma, age six months. He was a member of the Baptist clergy. During the Civil War, he enlisted in "B" Company, 89th Indiana Infantry, on August 8,1862 as a chaplain, and on August 17, 1862, he was commissioned into the Field & Staff, 12th Indiana Infantry. He mustered out of the military on June 8, 1865 in Washington DC. After the war, Gage wrote the regimental history of the 12th Indiana Infantry, "From Vicksburg to Raleigh," which was published 1923. By 1870, Reverend Gage was a Baptist minister living in Junction City, Davis County, Kansas, with his wife Mary and his children Mary, Sarah, Hattie, and Charles. By 1880, the Gage family had added another member, Calvin C. Gage, and resided in Slate Range, Yuba County According to the US 1880 Federal Census, Gage had been working as a school teacher for seven months at the time the census was taken. In 1900, Gage was a widower living in Monterey, and in 1908, he married his second wife, Alpha Drew, in Santa Monica. Gage died April 13, 1912 at the age of 84 and is buried at Oak Hill Memorial Park San Jose, Santa Clara County, California. *(Sources: 1860 US Federal Census; Report of the US Civil War Solider Records; Adjutant General of the State of Indiana; FIndaGrave.com; California, County Birth, Marriage, Death Records, 1849-1980. Photo: Moses Dwight Gage 1912, https://www.ancestry.com/mediaui-viewer/tree/6863521/person/ 6020294258/ media/af8ea6e3-5451-43d9-8dd0-de01b3805b3d? _phsrc=DNr10&_phstart=success)*

GODFREY, ERNEST

Ernest Godfrey was born on September 16 1876 in California. His father was from Vermont, and his mother was a Californian. In 1910, he was single and lived in a boarding house in Downieville. He was working in a placer mine. The boarding house was operated by Miles G. Calvin and his family, who also lived in Camptonville, and several other boarders also had ties to Camptonville: his brother Fred O. Godfrey Reuben Halkyard, Frank W Parlin, Joseph Tioni (who also died in the Brandy City Burn), Amaziah Trueworthy Ernest's parents were Noah L.

Godfrey and Margaret Nuttall. His maternal grandparents were John Nuttall, who was born in England, and Catherine Nuttall, who was born in Ireland. Ernest's mother was Camptonville resident's John D. Nuttall's sister. Godfrey died in 1915 in the Brandy City Burn and is burred in Camptonville Cemetery. *(Sources: US Federal Census 1880, 1900, 1910)*

GOOD TEMPLARS

The International Order of the Good Templars was one of several lodge organizations modeled on Freemasonry with similar rituals and regalia. The Good Templars differed from other organizations in that it allowed men and women equally to its membership and made no distinctions by race. It began in Utica, New York, by combining two lodges of the Knights of Jericho, another of the many fraternal organizations designed to foster temperance and abstinence in the 19th century. Daniel Cady founded one of the lodges in Utica, New York, in 1850, and Wesley Bailey founded the other in Castor Hollow, New York, in 1951. Daniel Cady was a well respected lawyer and judge who had served in the New York State legislature. He was also the father of Elizabeth Cady Stanton. suffragist, social activist, and abolitionist. The two lodges joined under the name of the Order of Good Templars, taking as their motto, "Friendship, Hope and Charity". A Grand Lodge was established in 1852 The organization spread rapidly in the US and Canada and in 1868 was established in England, The group established its lodges throughout the world during the later part of the 19th century and remained active with various attempts at modernization until at least 1979. *(Source: "International Order of Good Templars," Wikipedia.com;)*

In a letter to the *Marysville Daily Appeal* on November 24, 1876, Camptonville resident Reverend M.D. Gage wrote,

> The Good Templars have a flourishing organization here, owning a hall centrally located, which has recently been put in an attractive condition by papering the walls in panel work, painting the ceiling in gloss white, and graining the doors, window casings and wainscoting. The

> Lodge numbers over sixty members, including many of our most worthy citizens. At the recent installation the following officers were duly installed by D. G. W. Chief Templar Joseph Kerwin: W. C. T.. M. D. Gage ; W. V. T., Emma Gage ; W. S., B. I'. Hugg ; W. F. S., Frank Calvin ; W.T., C. M. Verrill ; W.M., C. Stroud ; W. I. G., Ella Gage; W. O. G., Wm. Groves. We occupy the Good Templars Hall for our Sunday services and Sabbath School, both being well attended. Our people, therefore, have ail the facilities for enjoying life ordinarily found in towns of this size

HALL, ELMER STARK ROBINSON

Elmer Stark Robinson Hall was born on March 29, 1880, on the ranch owned by his father Thomas J. Hall in Cache Creek, near Rumsey in Yolo County, the oldest of four children. Elmer Hall attended school in San Francisco, and then farmed land near Brownsville in Yuba County. He worked for the PG&E Company building the dam on Lake Francis. In 1900 he worked on the Dobbins ranch, and in 1904, Hall took a job on the Colgate project. He worked there until he was named the caretaker of the saw mill in Camptonville in 1912. Elmer S.R. Hall died in 1942 and is buried in the Camptonville Cemetery. "Do you know why I remember Elmer Hall? He had a peg leg. He lost his leg because of a runaway horse on the Main Street. He got run over by the wagon. In my lifetime he was the caretaker of the old PG&E mill property, if you know where that is. That's out beyond the Green Mailbox, you know, where Mrs. (Elma) Davis has her place, beyond Pendola Ranch where Mill Creek canyon is at the headwaters of Mill Creek. That's where the PG&E mill was. He was the caretaker there for years, and that mailbox where the road takes out wasn't a post office mailbox; it was his mailbox, and he painted it green so that location is always called the Green Mailbox. People would pick up his mail in town and leave it there. He used to keep a record of the rainfall and things like that." *(Source: Leland Pauly, The Camptonville Connection. Hank Meals)*

HORWEGE, WILLIAM

William Horwege was born in about 1872 in California. In 1880, he lived in Slate Range, a step-son of the household head Peter J. Mangel, the husband of his mother Margaretha. Peter Mangel came from Hamburg, Germany, and was a miner. William's father was born in Hanover, Germany, as was his mother. He had a brother and a sister: Lizzie aged 17 and John Henry aged four. In 1900, he lived with his mother and brother Henry, and he worked as a timber man. In 1910, William still lived in Slate Range and had a gold mine. He had Charles Whittum, later a Forest Ranger, as a boarder in his rented home. By 1920, William was working as a stage driver and owned his own home. He died in 1920 and is buried in Camptonville Cemetery. *(Sources: Sacramento Union, Number 37, 6 April 1920. US Federal Census; California Death Index 1905-1939; Camptonville Cemetery records)*

YUBA STAGE DRIVER MEETS SUDDEN DEATH

Special to the Union. MARYSVILLE, Yuba Co., April 5-. William Horwege, pioneer stage driver of Yuba county, dropped dead early Sunday morning at Dobbins, near here as the result of a stroke of apoplexy. He had been driving the stage carrying parcel and mail between Dobbins and Camptonville and had gone to the barn Sunday morning (April 4) to hitch up his team preparatory to leaving for Camptonville when he dropped dead in the barn. He was 48 years of age and a native of California. He was not married. He leaves one sister, Mrs. Lizzie King of Camptonville and two brothers, Jordan H. Horwege of Goldfield and John Horwege of Toll Station.

HOUGHTAILING, EDWARD

Edward Houghtailing was born in 1832 in New York. By 1870 he was living in Slate Range and working as a miner. Acton Cleveland writes he was Justice of the Peace at one time. He is buried in Camptonville Cemetery. *(Sources: US Federal Census;*

Morning Union, Nevada City, 1 February 1913)

ED. HOUGHTAILING DEAD

Edward Houghtailing, one of the oldest and best known residents of Camptonville, died there last Saturday and the funeral took place at Camptonvillc Monday. Deceased was over 80 years of age and was a man who gained the good will of all through his kindly ways. He was formerly justice of the peace at Camptonville and also managed the hotel there during the regime of W. B. Meek.

JONES, DR. CARL POWER

Dr. Carl P. Jones graduated in 1907 from the Cooper Medical College of San Francisco. His brother George L. Jones was the district attorney of Nevada County. The feisty Dr. Jones was involved in an "uproar" at a health board meeting in Grass Valley during which he punched another doctor in the mouth for describing one of his statements as a lie. The meeting had been called to investigate charges that cases of measles in the city were not being reported and that the quarantine was not being enforced. Dr. Jones, who was summoned to attend the meeting, was the only doctor in the city who was not a member of the Board of Health. A Dr. Brown asked him if he had not said that members of the board were not reporting measles cases, and Dr. Jones denied this but admitted he said that some physicians in the city were not reporting cases. "Brown asked him if Jones did not say that no member of the board of health could visit his cases. Jones stated that he did not wish other physicians to visit his cases unless in his company. Brown replied that he had cases enough of his own without resorting to such methods. Jones retorted with 'You did it once when your face was slapped.' 'Your brother said that and he lied,' said Brown. 'You went back on the statement when I asked you about it in the street,' replied Jones. "You lie!" came the answer from Brown. That was too much for Jones, who then took the punch. "The meeting broke up for a short time, but when order was restored it was decided to order all cases of measles reported and the quarantine law enforced." In 1918, Dr. Jones accompanied two Santa Rose girls to join a group of 14 nurses training for service overseas in a naval base hospital on Mare Island. In 1942, Dr. Jones was building a private hospital in Grass Valley, which he hoped would become a "little Mayo." *(Sources: Sacramento Union, Number 78, 11 May 1907; Sacramento Union, Number 50, 19 August 1911; Press Democrat, Volume XLV, Number 137, 28 September 1918; Mill Valley Record, Volume XLIV, Number 18, 6 March 1942)*

KIDDER, JOHN FLINT

John Flint Kidder was born June 2, 1830 in New York City. He was the son of Levi Kidder and Elvira (Parker) Kidder and the brother of Elmira J. Kidder Both of his parents were from Massachusetts. After graduating from Rensselaer University in 1847, he became the city engineer of Syracuse, New York, as well as superintendent of streets for some years. He moved to Carson City, Nevada, in 1860, and then to Portland, Oregon, where he engineered and built part of the Northern Pacific Railroad, surveying and superintending the construction of the line from Kalama, Washington for some 60 miles. He also worked under contract to locate the Nevada County Narrow Gauge Railroad from Colfax to Grass Valley. In 1876, he was named superintendent of the railroad, which was incorporate in 1874. When a new charter went into effect, Kidder bought the line. He was elected on the Republican ticket as the representative from El Dorado County to the state legislature in 1866. He was linked to the Masonic Lodge of Syracuse, New York, and took the Royal Arch degree, also belonging to the Ancient Order of United Workmen of Grass Valley. He married Sarah Ann Clark in 1873. In 1880 he was living in Grass Valley, California, with his wife Sarah A. Clark Kidder. They had one adopted daughter, Beatrice (Kidder) Ward Hubert (1885-1965).From 1884, he served as president of the Nevada County Narrow Gauge Railroad. He died in 1901. Kidder was originally buried at the Odd Fellows Masonic Cemetery in Grass Valley before his remains were brought to San Francisco and then to the Colma Columbarium. *(Sources: Encyclopedia of American Biography, 1800-1902; US Federal Census; Find A Grave Index, 1600s-Current)*

KIDDER, SARAH ANN CLARK

Sarah Ann Kidder was born on July 23,1842, in Iowa, and died on September 29, 1933 at the age of 91. Her father was Joshua Clark, an Oregon pioneer. She married John Flint Kidder in May of 1873. After the death of her husband in 1901, she became the first woman to run a railroad. She served in that position from 1901 to 1913. (While Acton Cleveland writes that it was J.F. Kidder who gave Bill Meek the "railroad rails from the old track and trestle" to help rebuild the mercantile building after the 1908 fire, it may have been Sarah Kidder who supplied these materials, since J.F. died in 1901. The rails could have been provided at some time before this, but Acton's writing suggests they were given after the fire. – Ed.) *(Sources: FindAGrave.com; US Federal Census)*

KING, CHARLES "CHARLEY" WILLIAM

Charles William King was born in 1886 and died in 1954. His parents were Edwin Gardner King, a miner, and Elizabeth "Lizzie" Horwege King, both born in California. He is buried in Camptonville Cemetery. *(Sources: US Federal Census; U.S., Find A Grave Index, 1600s-Current)*

LABADIE, FRANCIS "FRANK" SEBASTIAN

Francis Sebastian Labadie was born May 9, 1861, at Indiana Ranch in Dobbins. His father was Peter Labadie, who was born in 1823 in Canada and lived in Clay, St. Joseph, Indiana, in 1850. His mother Margarette Millot Labadie was born in France about 1824, and was living with her husband in Clay in 1850. She arrived in New York on August 27. 1832, having traveled on the ship *Fredonia* from Le Havre, France. Peter and Margarette married in Michigan in 1842. From 1870 to 1880, the family farmed in Foster Bar. Francis had six brothers and three sisters. Peter died August 8, 1882 at Maple Springs Ranch in Yuba County. His burial is at Indiana Ranch Cemetery, along with other members of the Labadie family.

By 1910, Francis was married and farming in Gridley, Butte County, with his wife Rachael M. :Labadie. In 1930, She was born in Brown's Valley March 29,1869. Francis lived on Spring Street in Camptonville where he owned and managed the Hotel Francis. Francis died on January 12, 1932, in Sutter County, and Rachael died November 6, 1947, in Yuba County. The Labadies are buried in Sacred Heart Cemetery in Dobbins. *(Sources: YubaRoots; US Federal Census; New York Arrivals; US French Catholic Church Records (Drouin Collection), 1695-1954')*

(According to information provided on RootsWeb, Francis "built the cedar sawmill at Oregon Hill, where he conducted a lumber and mill business for twenty-five years, then selling out and locating in Camptonville. Here he purchased the Camptonville Hotel, the best hostelry in the region, remodeled it, and named it Hotel Francis." (Source: www.rootsweb.ancestry.com/ ~cagha/biographies/l/labadie-francis.txt)

LANDLORD LABADIE IMPROVES HIS HOTEL

F. S. Labadie, genial proprietor of the Francis hotel at Camptonville, is one of the most progressive landlords in the mountains. At an expense of several hundred dollars he has just completed a renovation of the office, dining room and parlors of the hotel. The walls and ceiling have been handsomely painted and decorated by a clever artist, while beautiful oil paintings also grace the walls. Last year Mr. Labadie erected a large pump house and water tower, in which is installed a gasoline engine, supplying pure mountain water the year round. All of the choice fruits and vegetables used on the table are grown in the gardens which surround the hotel, while Mr. Labadie also maintains his own dairy. People passing to and from the mountains are always assured of a cordial welcome at the hands of Landlord Labadie *(Source: Morning Union, Nevada City, 1 July 1915)*

ADVERTISEMENT THE FRANCIS HOTEL, 1915

Hotel Francis Camptoinville Stop there going

or coming from the mountains. Home-like meals. Pine rooms. Fresh vegetables and fruits used on our table, grown in our own garden. Pure mountain water from our own tower and pump house. Central point of Nevada City and Downieville. Marysville and Camptonville, Pike City and the Brandy City stage and auto lines. F. S. LABADIE PROP. *(Source: Morning Union, 2 September 1915)*

LAZOVSKI. STANLEY JOSEPH

Stanley Lazovski was born on May 6, 1890, in Minsk, Russia. His parents were Joseph and Micholina Lazovsky. He arrived in New York, New York, in May 1910. He became a naturalized citizen of the United States in Pennsylvania in December 1923 stating his age as 33. He died on December 15, 1943 and is buried in the Camptonville Cemetery. *(Sources: US Social Security Applications and Claims Index, 1936-2007; Pennsylvania, Federal Naturalization Records, 1795-1931)*

LEWIS, DAVID "DAVE"

Dave Lewis was born in Wales in 1862. He came to the United States in 1886 and became a naturalized citizen. His physical description in the California voter registration for Sierra County in 1898 stated he had black hair and blue eyes. In 1910 he was single, lived on Freemans Road and worked as a gold miner. In 1930 he was single and lived in a house he owned on Spring Street in Camptonville and working at odd jobs. He had no radio. He died in 1939 and is buried in the Camptonville Cemetery. His headstone inscription reads "Mason." *(Sources: US Federal Census; FindAGrave.com; California Voter Registration Great Register).*

LEWIS, FRANCIS "FRANK"

Frank Lewis was born in Wales in 1842. He immigrated to the United States in 1864. In his California voter registration for Sierra County in June 1898 in Pike City, he is described as having hazel eyes and grey hair with "coal marks" on his left cheek; coal marks were small pieces of coal embedded in the skin of miners that came from the force of explosions in the mine to loosen the coal; they were described as blue in color and similar to tattoos. He married in 1870 and became a naturalized citizen in 1871 in Downieville. In 1900, he lived in Forest in Sierra County and worked as a mine foreman. In 1910, he was living on Celestial Valley Road with Margaret, his wife of 41 years who was also born in Wales, and working in a gold mine. He died on December 21, 1911. He is buried in the Camptonville Cemetery where his headstone reads "Mason." *(Sources: US Federal Census; California Voter Registration Great Register; FindAGrave.com)*

LIPP & SULLIVAN

This business is located on site of the home of Acton's great-uncle Jason R. Meek in "the old Casey Block" (the corner of 5th and D) in Marysville. The Lipp & Sullivan building was originally located on the north side of 5th Street between E and High Streets. It was the home of the owner of Garrett Wholesale Grocery Company. Garrett sold it to Kelly Brothers Funeral Directors, the firm that became Lipp & Sullivan Funeral Directors in 1928. .In 1940, the house was moved to its present location. It still contains the grand staircase and all the original rooms. *(Source: Lipp & Sullivan website)*

LORD, DR. FREDRICK KING

My father, Frederick King Lord, was born in Waupaca, Wisconsin while the family was there on a visit. My father led a rather interesting life in his early days, doing some prospecting. He was a Wells Fargo agent in Nevada City, California, for a short time but retired from that saying it was a little too dangerous a life for him. He then went to San Francisco and studied medicine at what was then known as Cooper Medical College and which is now the Cooper College of Medicine of Stanford University. He took his post graduate work at Louisville Medical School and while there met and married my mother, Lizzie Moyer. The Moyers were originally from England, then through Switzerland and Holland to the United States, arriving in Pennsylvania area in the 1600s.My father then went back to San Francisco and persuaded Southern Sierra Power Company of the need for a doctor in Northern California. This company later became Pacific Gas Electric which had mining and timber interests in the north. Dr. Lord practiced medicine in Port Wine, Brownsville and Camptonville, California for many years. His second wife, Virginia Pearl Meek, was the daughter of William Bull Meek who was one of the leading figures in that part of the country. There were three children by the first marriage. Leah Moyer Lord died at an early age, Loren Waldauer Lord and myself. Virginia and Dr. Lord had two children, John Frederick Lord and a daughter who died in infancy. *(Source: Otho Lord, 1993)*

MARQUARDT, LOUIS

Lou Marquardt, who served as constable in Camptonville for some years, was born January 17, 1892 in California. When he registered for the draft in World War I on June 5, 1917, he stated that he was working for Dave Humphrey on Mill Creek as a farm laborer. According to his World War I draft registration card, which he filled out on June 5, 1917, he was born on January 17, 1892. On the card his is described as single, stout, tall, and partially bald. What hair he had was brown, as were his eyes. He also registered for the World War II draft in 1942. By this time, he was married and working at the Oak Valley Lumber Mill. He died on July 23, 1956, According to Leland Pauly, Louis Marquardt was the brother of Mrs. Turner, Mrs. Humphreys, and Mrs. Sommer. He had a ranch on Mill Creek and used to drive the Mill Creek school bus. "I can remember he bought a brand new 1932 Chevrolet touring car. You didn't see many touring cars after the Twenties. He was a brother to all of those people over on Mill Creek. He was a bachelor until later years when he got married." Leland said. *(Sources: The Camptonville Connection by Hank Meals; US Federal Census)*

MARTIGNONE. ANDREW

Andrew Martignone was born in Genoa, Italy, about 1852. By 1900, he had been in the United States for some 20 years, was a naturalized citizen and was married and making his home in Slate Range, Yuba County, and working as a miner. In 1900, he and his wife Antoinette Mary Caposie Martignone, who was born in Italy On September 20, 1870, had a child, John, age 7. John Martignone died in 1920 and is buried in Camptonville Cemetery. Andrew had another son, Marion William Martignone, who was born in Marysville. Andrew died om 1924 at the age of 72. Antoinette died on March 27, 1949, in Yuba County, at age 89.. They are both buried in Camptonville Cemetery. *(Sources: US Federal Census; Camptonville Cemetery records)*

MARTIGNONE, MARION WILLIAM

Marion William Martignone was born in Marysville in 1903. His parents were Andrew (Andrea) and Antoinette Martignone. Marion's World War II draft card lists his birth date as June 20, 1903. Marion married Mildred J Hauton in Vancouver, Washington, on September 15, 1938. When he registered for the draft in Oak Valley on February 14, 1942, he was living in Klamath Falls, Oregon, and working for Klamath Machine and Locomotive. He died in Oregon in September 1956. *(Sources: US Social Security Death Index, 1935-2014; US Federal Census; World War II Draft Cards Young Men, 1940-1947)*

MASSA, ANDREW JOSEPH, "ANDY"

Andrew Massa was born in Italy October 2, 1873. He is buried in Camptonville Cemetery. He immigrated to the United States in 1877 or 1878. He was a naturalized citizen. In 1900, Andrew lived in Lincoln, Sierra County, with his mother Madalena Massa, also born in Italy about 1848, and his brother Francis "Frank" (August16, 1886-April 14, 1970), age 13. He was working as a laborer in a mine. In 1910, he was living in Downieville with his widowed mother and brothers Albert Massa (April 9, 1878-March 14, 1961), and Frank John Massa. He was a naturalized citizen and worked in a placer mine. In 1920, the family owned a farm in Downieville. In 1930, Andrew was still single, living and working in Liberty, Siskiyou County, in a placer mine. He died in 1940. *(Sources: US Federal Census; Camptonville Cemetery records)*

MAYO, ORIN, GEORGE "BILL"

Orin George Mayo was born in 1827 in Maine. In 1880, he lived alone in Slate Range and worked as a carpenter. At the time of the 1880 US Federal Census, he had been unemployed for ten months. His 1881 California Voter Registration listed his home as Sierra County. The Mayo family appears to have been fairly prominent in Maine. *(Sources: US Federal Census; California, Voter Registers, 1866-1898; Message Board, ancestry.com; Sacramento Bee October 23, 1903)*

PASSING OF A PIONEER AT CAMPTONVILLE

MARYSVILLE, Oct 23, 1903- Orin George Mayo, an old and respected citizen of Camptonville, Yuba County, died at his home at that place Wednesday after an illness extending over a period of several months of dropsy. He was a native of Maine, aged 75 years, and resided in Camptonville may years, but had no family. Mr. Mayo was familiarly spoken of as "Bill" and he was a genial clever gentleman who had friends wherever known. At the date of his death, he was conducting a hotel and saloon, but had not been able to give the business personal attention for some time. During many years past he had been closely identified with the industries and business interests of the town, and he will be greatly missed. *(Sacramento Bee 10/23/1903)*

According to Leland Pauly, "He was a friend of Bill Meek's. Bill built that Mayo Building for him after the fire. It was a bar, but of course, nothing much thrived after the fire, and when prohibition came in, it was an ice cream parlor for a little while when I was a kid. Mayo had it, along with Goldthwait. I was really too small to remember any details on it, but I remember being able to get ice cream. You understand there was no electricity here so they had to use ice until bottle gas came in in the thirties." *(Source: The*

Camptonville Connection, Hank Meals)

MEEK, JOHN ROBERT

John Robert Meek was Acton Cleveland's great-grandfather. He was born on July 26,1820, in La Chien, Canada, and baptized in 1824 in Saint Gabriel Presbyterian Church. His mother, Elizabeth (McCaw) Meek was born in 1789 and died in 1842 in Tallahatchie, Mississippi. His father James Meek was born in 1789 and died in York, South Carolina, in 1844. One source says John Robert Meek married Caroline Barber Bull, born July 4, 1822 and died November 5, 1898, in San Francisco in 1854, but another says they married in Marysville Caroline was originally from Canada but later moved with her family to Connecticut before coming to California. John R. Meek traveled to California by ship in 1851 and started is merchandising career in Downieville and Indian Valley in 1855 before moving to Camptonville. John R. Meek died on September 1,1906, in Camptonville and his buried with his wife in Camptonville Cemetery. *(Sources: US Federal Censuses; Delay, Peter, History of Yuba County, 1924).*

MEEK, WILLIAM BULL

William Bull Meek was born on December 25, 1857, and died on January 23, 1936, at the age of 79. He is buried in Camptonville Cemetery.

MAYOR OF CAMPTONVILLE HAS MULTITUDINOUS DUTIES

During all the agonies of poverty and the joys of success that have occurred to the town one man has remained at the helm with varying fortunes, and that man is W. B. Meek, who owns most of the town and has varied and useful occupations. He is proprietor of the hotel, livery stable, general merchant, Wells-Fargo agent, notary public, owner of the town water works, master of the lodges, proprietor of the saloon and also of the Good Templars Hall, undertaker, town preacher at funerals in the absence of the regular minister, banker, butcher, Fourth of July orator, spring poet, school trustee, street superintendent, and general entertainer of all pilgrims who visit Camptonville, and his hospitality is known from one end of the state to the other. *(Source: Sacramento Union, Number 8, 1 September 1907)*

MAKES THRILLING DASH.

Special to the Union. NEVADA CITY (Nevada Co.). May 13. — The days of the thrilling moments for stage drivers and passengers have not altogether vanished. When "Big Bill" Meek of Camptonville takes the line and drives his four between Goodyear s Bar and Downieville there is something is likely to happen at any moment. When the spot in the Yuba canyon was reached yesterday the passengers were surprised to find the river running several feet deep in the road at the turn. It was evident that they would receive a drenching if an attempt was made to drive through the water. Meek threw out the mail sacks and advised his passengers to alight. This they did without hesitation and they climbed the hill and went around above the turn where the water covered the road, carrying the mail sacks with them. Cracking his whip. Meek urged his horses into the swollen river, and they plunged. The water covered the floor of the stage, and the horses almost lost their footing, but they made the other side in safety, and the journey was resumed. The Downieville residents were much surprised to see the stage come in that day. *(Source: Sacramento Union, May 14, 1915)*

100 YEARS AGO IN NEVADA COUNTY: NOVEMBER 1914

W.B. Meek of Camptonville, searching through and old cabin, found an oddity — an 1853 coin that also had half that year's calendar stamped on it *(Source: https://www.theunion.com/news/ local-news/100-years-ago-in-nevada-county-november-1914/)*

W.B. MEEK OBITUARY

CAMPTONVILLE, Yuba Co., Jan 24, (1936) – William Bull Meek, 79, pioneer stage driver, former Yuba County assessor, local merchant, Wells Fargo agent, Clamper and authority on California history, is dead at his home here. Death came last night as the result of a long illness and age … *(Source: Sacramento Bee, January 24,1936)*

W.B. MEEK OBITUARY

William Bull Meek, pioneer knight of the whip, merchant, justice of the peace, hail fellow well met, until years overcame his stubborn vitality, has gone to his final reward. Born and reared midst the roughness of the mining days of Yuba County mountains, an authority on the gold trails, no one can replace him. *(Source: Marysville Appeal-Democrat, January 27, 1936)*

MEEK. JASON RUSSELL

Jason R. Meek was born in Marysville on July 5, 1854, to John R. and Caroline Bull Meek. He attended public schools in Indian Valley with his brother William Bull Meek. He attended McGill University in Montreal, Canada, taking courses in civil engineering and returned to California in 1876. He became Yuba County surveyor in 1877 and served in that role for many years. He married Christine E. Freese of California, and they had five children: Alice M. who married O.L. Gray, the dredge master of Oakland; Donald; Caroline, a trained nurse; and Jason R. Jr., who served with the American Expeditionary Force in World War I. *(Source: Thompson and West)*

MONDADA, PETER

Records show Peter Mondada was born in Switzerland in either

1849 or 1852. He came to the United States in 1874 and became a naturalized citizen. He was single and worked as an engineer/miner in a gold mine. In 1910, he lived on Celestial Valley Road and was a gold miner. He was still single and a miner in 1925. He died in Nevada County on October 6 in 1925. He is buried in Camptonville Cemetery. *(Sources: US Federal Census; Camptonville Cemetery records)*

NATHAN DOHRMANN COMPANY

Acton Cleveland noted that the Clark brothers, Charley and Frank, were associated with the Nathan Dohrmann Company, which sold china. This is a photo of the company building at Geary and Stockton in San Francisco in August 17, 1935. *(Source: Photo: Gabriel Moulin (1872-1945); San Francisco History Center San Francisco Public Library_)*

NUTTALL, JOSEPH DANIEL

Joseph Daniel Nuttall was born in 1860 in California. He died in 1929. His wife Mary Ann Butz Nuttall was born in 1865 and died in 1919. They are both buried in Camptonville Cemetery, along with Joseph's brother Johnnie W. Nuttall (January 7, 1856-October 4, 1872). In 1890, the family is recorded in the US Federal Census as living in "North East, Yuba, California" with Strawberry Valley listed as their post office. He was working as a miner. By 1910, he was married and living on Oak Valley Road with his wife Mary, sons Frederick Peter and John R., and daughters Mary K. and Pearl L. He lived on a farm and owned a gold mine. In 1920, he was widowed and living in Alameda with his son John and daughter Pearl. He died in 1929 and is buried in Camptonville Cemetery. *(Sources: Camptonville Cemetery Records; US Federal Census 1880, 1910, 1920; US Social Security Applications and Claims Index, 1936-2007; California County Birth, Marriage, and Death Records, 1849-1980)*

PACIFIC COAST SYRUP COMPANY

Acton Cleveland remembers Charley "Dirty Shirt" Clark

working as a salesman for the Pacific Coast Syrup Company in San Francisco. The company got its start in 1900 when W.A. England and H.D. Skellinger founded the Eng-Skell Company. In the early days, the company made only a few products, chiefly flavoring extracts for the bakery and bottling industries. They also made ginger brandy and orange bitters for the bar trade. The firm expanded its business in 1905 to include strawberries, pineapple, and bananas in its fountain fruit. The 1906 earthquake and Fire in San Francisco destroyed much of the plant, and its insurance company went bankrupt. However, the safe that contained the formulas, seal and ledger of the company was saved, which allowed the business to continue in a new location that same year. In 1907, the soda fountain was becoming popular, and the firm recognized its opportunity in providing crushed fruits, toppings and fountain syrups for the trade. In 1912, it added soda fountains and equipment to its offerings. A Los Angeles branch opened in 1922. In 1930, the company built a large 100,000 square foot Art Deco building in the SOMA district of San Francisco designed by A.C. Griewark. Sales dropped by 40 percent during the Great Depression of the 1930s, but the company made a deal with a bank that allowed it to survive. In the 1930s and 1940s, the company added a bakery division and a complete line of soda fountains, ice cream cabinets, freezers, and store fixtures. During World War II, it shipped its products and fixtures to virtually every Army and Navy base in the Pacific war theater. By 1957, the company was selling 4,500 gallons of vanilla extract per year, and the 1966, it was doing more than $10 million in business with branches in Phoenix, Sacramento, Colton, Eureka, San Jose, Fresno and Reno. The company continues doing business s Esco Foods Inc. and in 2004 created a website to sell directly to the consumer. *(Sources: Esco https://www.escofoods.com/about-us.html)*

PAGNELLO, WARD EDMUND

This could be Ward Edmund Pagnello who was born in California on July 4, 1890. He was married and worked as a clerk on the railroad. In 1900 he lived in Alameda with his parents Edmond H. Pagnello who was born in Canada and Jessie M. Smith Pagnello who was born in Alturas, California. In 1920 he lived with his family in Washington, Yolo County, at the home of his mother-in-law Annie Edwards. He worked as a clerk in a "railroad shop." In 1930 he was living in Sacramento with his wife Annie and their two children. He died on February 27, 1941, in San Francisco. *(Sources: US Federal Census; California Death Index, 1940-1997; US Social Security Applications and Claims Index, 1936-2007)*

PARLIN, FRANK W.

The Parlins can trace their ancestry back to the first tribes in the Scottish Highlands and have an extensive history in Maine. Frank W. Parlin's father Levi Fletcher Parlin was born on May 13, 1823, in Concord, Maine. He married his first wife Mrs. Sarah "Sally" (Richardson) Bickford of Gardner, Maine, who was born June 15, 1818,. Levi was a merchant in East Machias, Maine, until 1851 when the couple moved to California. By 1852,he was living in Clipper Mills and working as a hotel keeper. Frank was born September 2, 1857, and his mother Sarah died October 4, 1857, in Woodleaf, Yuba County. By 1860, Frank, his brother, two sisters and his father were living in Brandy City. Levi married his second wife Sylvania Taylor who was born in August 1843 in Missouri. in 1865; they had two children. Levi died September 11, 1907, in Oroville. Sylvania died on May 31, 1915, in Butte County and is buried in the Old Oroville Cemetery. In 1870, Frank was attending school in Marysville. In 1890, he was registered to vote in Sierra County and listed his local residence as Mountain House. In 1900, Frank lived in Butte County at a boarding house and worked as a lumberman. In 1910, he was a boarder in Downieville and worked as a placer miner. By 1930, Frank was living in the Odd Fellows Home in Saratoga. He died on November 12, 1931 in San Jose and is buried at the Saratoga IOOF Cemetery. *(Sources: US Federal Census; North America Family Histories, 1500-2000; The Parlin genealogy. The descendants of Nicholas Parlin of Cambridge, Mass by Frank Edson Parlin, 1860-1939). 1913)*

PHELAN, MRS. BERTHA

Bertha Phelan was married to Earnest Phelan, the son of California pioneers Evan and Sarah Derrick Phelan, Evan and Sarah (Derrick) Phelan, natives of Arkansas and Missouri respectively, Evan Phelan came to California in 1857 and started a cattle ranch. Sarah crossed the plains in 1855. By 1887, the family had moved to Oregon House where they purchased an old hotel property. According to Peter Delay (1920), "The hotel is conducted in a first-class manner, and is located twenty-seven miles northeast of Marysville on the Camptonville cross-roads." Earnest Phelan was born on January 2, 1880, in Penryn, Placer County. Bertha was born in California about 1884 and lived with the Phelan family in Parks Bar in 1900 and 1910. Earnest died by drowning in a dredging accident in 1918 at the Kentucky Ranch. *(Sources: US Federal Census)*

POLLEY, ELNATHAN NELSON

Elnathan Polley, who is buried in the Camptonville Cemetery, was born on July 17, 1837, in New York. He died on March 19, 1911, in Chico, California, at the age of 73. He was the son of Amos Polley and Dorothy (Ault) Polley. According to information at http://www.findagrave.com supplied by Mrs. Jessie Polley, E.N. Polley was married, his death certificate noted his burial in Camptonville, and it is likely, given his first name, that he is descended from Elnathan Polley Sr. of Massachusetts. According to the 1850 US Federal Census, E.N. Polley, age 11, was living with his parents, two sisters, and two brothers in Massena, Saint Lawrence, New York. According to Leland Pauly, "He was a business man who had something to do with Brandy City," *(Sources: The Camptonville Connection by Hank Meals; US Federal Census of 1850).*

PORTER, GEORGE F.

George Porter was born about 1860 and died in 1912. He is buried in the Browns Valley Cemetery in Yuba County. The inscription on his headstone reads " Here is a woodsman of the world." *(Sources: FindAGrave.com; US Federal Census)*

RITCHIE, JEFF

According to the 1860 US Federal Census, Jeff Ritchie was born about 1830 in Georgia. He was living near Camptonville and working as a miner. *(Source: US Federal Census)*

ROMARGI, MADAME

The story of the Romargi family of Florida House is both legendary and elusive. In the 1880s, everyone seemed to know about their nefarious doings with highwaymen, bandits, and unsavory characters of all kinds at the stopping place they ran on the Henness Pass Road. Pinning down any confirmable facts – even the most basic like their real names - is difficult, however. The editor has found several spellings of the name Romargi, for example, so it's unclear what the "real" one is. W.B. Meek provides the most reliable information as he knew Madame Romargi personally. While it is commonly believed that Mrs. Romargi was an Italian gypsy from Florida, the 1880 US Federal Census says she was born in South Carolina. John Romargi, also listed in the 1880 census, is listed as coming from Sardinia. The family, which included two grandchildren, Algernon and Jennie, was living in Indian Hill in Sierra County in 1880. Contemporary newspaper accounts veer toward the salacious, which makes for great reading but questionable fact.

The following information is presented with the warning that we shouldn't let facts get in the way of a good story.

> Madame Romargi, husband John, son and daughter Jane ran a stopping place on the Henness Pass Road in Sierra County known variously as the Florida House or the Sierra Nevada House from sometime in the 1860s until it was destroyed by fire in May 1888. The place had a notorious history ,known chiefly as a place where bandits, highwaymen, and other outlaws took refuge. Her grandson Algie died in Folsom Prison. According to the California Voters Register, John Romargi was born in 1816. There are numerous contemporary newspaper accounts of shootings and brawling at the Romargi's Florida House hotel and saloon, but few facts are available about Madame Romargi herself. It is believed she was of Italian gypsy ancestry and is always described as being very rough and tough. Leland Pauly said she and her husband came from Florida where he had an organ grinder act and worked

with a monkey. *(Sources: US Federal Censes; Personal conversation with Leland Pauly, 2002; Henness Pass Road Tour Guide)*

ROTHE, NICHOLAS "NICK"

Nicholas Rothe was born on October 17, 1879, in Dubno, Russia. He came to the United States in 1895. In 1935, he lived in Camptonville. According to his WWII draft registration card, he was living in Camptonville in 1942. He and his wife Marguerite Salathe had three children: Henry M., Emi S., and Florence I. The 1930 US Federal Census shows the family living in Alameda, where Nick was working as a fireman at a nursery. This census information lists his parents as coming from Austria. His wife Marguerite was born in 1879 in Switzerland and died in March 1974 in Yuba County. Her father was Swiss and her mother was German. Both she and Nick were naturalized American citizens. In 1940, the couple lived on a ranch in Garden Valley. Nick and Marguerite were the grandparents of Paul Pauly, Leland Pauly's nephew. Their daughter Florence was Paul's "Aunty Flo." Nick died in 1962 and is buried in Camptonville Cemetery. *(Sources: US Social Security Applications and Claims Index,1936-2007; US Federal Census; FindAGrave.com: Camptonville Cemetery Records; Interview with Paul Pauly in Camptonville, California, September 4. 2017)*

RUSSELL, PETER HENRY

Peter Henry Russell was born sometime between 1827. According to his California voter registrations, he lived in Camptonville from 1880 to at least 1896. His listing in 1885 stated he was a miner. Russell was originally from Ireland and became a naturalized citizen on April 24, 1867, in Yuba County. In 1884, Russell owned the Honeycomb Mine, which was located about three miles from Camptonville on John Ramm's ranch, in partnership with C.W. Cross of Nevada City. The quartz mine was an old one that had not shown much promise and had not been worked for some time, but Russell and Cross attained very good results there. They set up a five-stamp mill that crushed ten tons per day and recovered substantial amounts of rich ore.

(Sources: US Federal Census; California State Court Naturalization

Records 1850-1986; Morning Union, Volume 35, Number 4545, 21 October 1884)

SHARP, DAN

Acton identifies Dan Sharp as his cousin. He was the manager of the S.G. Dry Goods Company in Marysville. Daniel Lawrence Sharp was born in August 1872 in California. In 1880, he lived in Slate Range, Yuba County, with his father, John Sharp who came from Wisconsin, and his mother Ellen J. Sharp who came from Kentucky. Also living in the household were his brother Charles K. Sharp and his grandmother Elizabeth Spaulding. In 1890, Dan was living in a rooming house at 419 1/2 First Street in the 2nd Ward in Marysville and working in the dry goods business. By 1910, Dan, still single, was renting a house on 4th Street in the 3rd Ward in Marysville and was listed as the employer of a dry goods store. In 1920, still single and still running a dry goods business, Dan was listed in the Federal Census as the head of household on D Street in Marysville's 1st Ward. The household included 14 men, who were probably lodgers of Sharp. (Sources: US Federal Census 1880, 1910, 1920)

SIMS, JOSIAH

The Reverend Josiah Sims was born in Cornwall, England, on December 11, 1836. His father, who died when Sims was 12, had been a prosperous farmer; his mother was born into the aristocratic family Trevardon. Sims had a gift for public speaking when he gave a speech on "intemperance" that resulted in 99 people "taking the pledge" to abstain from alcohol. He spent three years studying theology, and once he gained admittance to the Methodist Church of England, he became known throughout England as "The Boy Preacher" and was in great demand. He married Mary Porley in England in 1857 He emigrated to America in 1866 and was pastor at several churches in New York State until he decided to go to California in 1872. He started as pastor in the Nevada City Congregational Church in June 1873. The church prospered under his leadership, and he was encouraged to enter politics. Initially hesitant to do so, Sims was elected to the State Assembly as a Republican and immediately began working toward and ultimately defeating a bill that would make hydraulic mining a felony. Sims was reelected in 1888 to a second term during which he was chair of the Committee on Public Morals and trustee of the reformatory in Whittier. He was a member of the Royal Arch Chapter of the Masonic order. In 1911, Reverend Sims celebrate his 30th year as pastor at the Congregational Church in Nevada City. *(Sources: A Memorial and Biographical History of Northern California, Illustrated: Containing a History of this Important Section of the Pacific Coast from the Earliest Period of Its Occupancy...and Biographical Mention of Many of Its Most Eminent Pioneers and Also of Prominent Citizens of Today. Lewis Publishing Company,1891,California; the Nevada City Union, June, 1911).*

SNOWDON HILL MINE

This mine was originally owned by Jeremiah Watts, who was the oldest Welsh pioneer in California at the time of his death in 1917. It was named for Snowdon, the highest mountain in Wales. It saw a resurgence in 1923 when it was again operated on an extensive scale. Watts owned the mine until 1909. He was a past master of the Gravel Range Lodge of Masons in Camptonville and was very interested in Welsh literature and poetry. At the Gorsedd, a meeting of contemporary Welsh bards held during the Panama–Pacific International Exposition world's fair held in San Francisco (February 20 to December 4, 1915), Watts was honored with a membership and the title of "Hen Bererin" (Old Pilgrim) in the organization. He died at the age of 90. His brother was Evan Watts, a well-known pioneer builder. *(Sources: Mariposa Gazette, Number 32, 13 January 1917; Santa Cruz Evening News, Volume 31, Number 55, 5 January 1923)*

STEPHENS, JOHN ALLEN

The birth date and birthplace of John Allen Stephens is uncertain. While his headstone in Camptonville Cemetery says he was born on June 24, 1865, and "Born in Ireland / There is rest in heaven," the US Federal Census for 1880 lists his birth date as about 1866 and his birthplace as Ohio. His mother, Ann, was born in Ireland, however, and his father was born in Kentucky. John had two brothers and one sister. He died on January 14, 1908. *(Sources: US Federal Census; FIndAGrave.com)*

Contemporary newspaper accounts of the Stephens/Horwege incident offer more detailed accounts of Stephen's death.

DIED AFTER A FIGHT
John Stevens and William Horwege Indulge in a Fatal Affray

.MARYSVILLE, Jan. 14.—About 3 o'clock this afternoon John Stevens, a well-known farmer of Camptonville, and a young man named Horwege, engaged in a fight as the result of a drinking bout. Stevens slapped Horwege in the face and the latter knocked Stevens down and began to choke him. When separated, the latter started for his horse and cart and proceeded to drive away, but had only gone a short distance when he was seen to fail out of the cart and when picked up he was dead. But little can be learned of the affair, other than above stated, but it is the general belief that death was primarily due to the rough treatment received during the affray. Coroner Kelly has asked the local justice of the peace to hold an inquest and Dr. Lord of Camptonville will perform an autopsy tomorrow. District Attorney Greely will leave for the scene to make an investigation. *(Source: Sacramento Union, Number 143, 15 January 1908)*

HAPPENINGS ALONG THE COAST

John Stephens, a farmer living near Camptonville, Yuba County, was killed during a fight with W. Horwege. The killing took place in front of Meeks' saloon. Stephens slapped Horwege on the face and Horwege choked him into insensibility. Notwithstanding this, after regaining consciousness Stephens arose, went down the street, entered his cart and started to drive off. He died within a few seconds. *(Source: "Late Happenings Along The Coast Interesting Items of News From Those States that Border the Broad Pacific. Current Events*

Among Your Neighbors In the Far West Gathered by Mail and Telegraph and Presented In Kalediosсopic Array." Lompoc Journal, Number 36, 25 January 1908.)

SULLIVAN, JEREMIAH PETER "JERRY"

Jerry Sullivan was born on July 5, 1888, in California. In 1910, he lived in Colusa with his parents Timothy and Bridget Sullivan, who were married in 1879 and were both from Ireland. They had a total of ten children, eight of whom were living. His father was the proprietor of a livery stable, having been working in that capacity at least since 1900 in Colusa. Jerry Sullivan had five brothers and two sisters. In 1920, Jerry was single and living with his brother. They were both working as undertakers in Colusa. In 1940,Jerry Sullivan was living in Marysville with his wife Pauline. He was a funeral home owner and director at Lipp & Sullivan. According to Acton Cleveland, he was the coroner for Yuba County in 1943. He died in 1963 and is buried In Sierra View Memorial Park in Yuba County *(Sources: FindAGrave.com; US Federal Census; US Social Security Applications and Claims Index, 1936-2007)*

TIONI, JOSEPH

Joseph Tioni was born in Italy in about 1874. He came to the US in 1891 and was a naturalized citizen. In 1910, Tioni was a widower and lived in a boarding house in Downieville operated by Miles G. Calvin. He worked as a miner in a placer mine. The other boarders included Miles Calvin, Sarah Calvin, Irene Calvin, Olive Calvin, Reuben Halkyard, Frank W Parlin, Amaziah Trueworthy, Edward Hansen, Fred O Godfrey, and Ernest E Godfrey died as a result of the Brandy City Burn on December 25, 1915. (*Sources: Camptonville Cemetery Records; US Federal Census; Camptonville Cemetery records)*

TRUEWORTHY, AMAZIAH HINCKLEY

According to the 1910 Federal Census, Trueworthy was living in the boarding house run by Miles G. Calvin in Downieville in

1910. He was born in Maine in 1847. The 1910 Census records him being "a wage earner," a carpenter "in the mines," and married for 42 years. His father was from Maine, and his mother was from Massachusetts. When the census taker came to call, Trueworthy had been out of work for one week. According to California Voter Registrations 1900-1968, he was born in 1839 and lived in Camptonville sometime between1900 and 1932. *(Sources: US Federal Census; California Voter Registrations 1900-1968)*

WAYMAN, THEODORE

Theodore Wayman was born about 1863 in California. In 1910, he lived on Freeman's Road on the property at Freeman's Crossing, which he bought from Ben Derickson, a nephew of Thomas Freeman. The original buildings burned down, and Wayman rebuilt the structures as they were until 1949. Wayman's parents were from Illinois. The rockaway carriage, named for the city of Rockaway, Queens, a fashionable beach resort in its day, was first made in 1830. It was a light and low horse-drawn vehicle with four wheels. It was popular with families in the US because it was enclosed and its roof extended over the front seat to provide protection from the weather.

The accident was described in the Sacramento Union as follows:

PLUNGE OVER GRADE FATAL FOR WAYMAN

Owner of Toll Road Dies in Automobile on Way to the Hospital.

OTHERS LUCKILY ESCAPE

Camptonville Party of Six Bound for Dance Roll 100 Feet—Only Two Hurt.

Special to the Union. NEVADA CITY (Nevada Co.), April 2.—Theodore Wayman, owner of Freeman's Crossing and toll road who was injured when the rig in which he was driving near Camptonville last night with a party of five others bound for a dance went over an embankment, died tonight a mile north of this city while being brought in an automobile to a local hospital. Wayman's back was dislocated, and he was paralyzed from the shoulders down.

The accident happened on the Oregon grade about 10 o'clock last night as Wayman was driving a party consisting of Gordon Kessler of Bullard's Bar, Misses Marguerite and Ida King, and Beatrice and Bernice Kendall of Camptonville to Pike City, Sierra County, to attend a dance. The night was exceedingly dark, and although Wayman had a headlight on the front of the rig, he could not see the road plainly.

A short distance below Kendall Ravine, the horses shied, and the rig with its occupants was suddenly precipitated over an embankment. The outfit struck a tree about fifty feet below the road. Miss Marguerite King was not so fortunate as the rest of the party and rolled fully fifty feet farther. One of the horses went the entire distance also and was so badly injured that it was dead when found this morning. The other animal was but slightly injured and was rescued this morning. Miss King was bruised considerably by the fall, but will soon be all right. She is exceedingly fortunate that she was not fatally injured or killed outright.

It was at once apparent that Wayman's injuries would probably prove fatal. One of the horses fell on him. dislocating his back and bruising him considerably. He did not lose consciousness, and talked to Louis Woods, Ralph Carpenter, Buzz Calahan and Charles King, who came to the party's rescue when they heard the screams of the men and women.

Wayman was rescued with difficulty and placed in Ralph Carpenter's wagon and taken to Camptonville. Dr. C. L. Miller of Nevada City was telephoned to, but being unable to go sent Dr. Fred Sprague of Grass Valley. He left in an auto for Camptonville and attempted to return here In time to save Wayman. He made an examination and found that Wayman's back was dislocated fully half an inch and that he was paralyzed from the shoulders down.

(Sources: http://www.aaqeastend.com/contents/portfolio/long-island-museum-carriage-collection-finest-collection-of-horse-drawn-vehicles/; US Federal Census; California Historical Quarterly, Vol. 28, No. 3, Sep., 1949; Sacramento Union, Number 41, 3 April 1911)

WHITE'S HOSPITAL

The White Hospital was located at 29th and J Streets in Sacramento, California. It was opened January 12, 1910, by Dr. John L. White. Dr. White was a physician, surgeon and served as Superintendent of the Sacramento County Hospital at one time. The hospital was built at a cost of $90,000 and included several four-bed wards and thirty private rooms. It could accommodate 50 patients. The main building was erected in 1910, and in 1911, an annex expanded the hospital's capacity from 50 to 85 patients. In 1912, the hospital charged $14 per week for a ward bed. $17.50 for a two-bed room, and between $3.00 and $5.00 per day for a private room. The hospital treated patients suffering from any ailment other than contagious diseases. It also offered a nurse education program that instructed 20 nurses at a time. After Dr. White was killed in March 1917 at the age of 41 in a head-on collision at the intersection of 21st and M Streets, his wife Camille F. White incorporated the hospital with herself as president and Florence Klacser as manager and secretary. The hospital closed in 1924. *(Source: Hospital pamphlet, Sacramento Room, Sacramento Public Library)*

WOLFF, JOHN G. "JACK"

John G. Wolff was born in California in October of 1865 or 1866. In 1870, John G Wolffe was four years old and lived in Sears, Downieville, Sierra County, with his parents, sister Caroline, age 8, and baby sister Mary. His father Jean Wolff, who came from France, was assessed for taxes in St. Louis, Sierra County, in 1864, 1865, and 1866, so John was probably born here. St. Louis is believed to have been the earliest mining town in northern Sierra

County. It was founded by a group of individuals from Missouri who were working the placer claims on a tributary of Slate Creek. In the 1850s, St. Louis was a lot like Camptonville, with more than 100 miners' cabins, several hotels, three saloons, a jewelry store, barber shop, Wells Fargo branch, sawmill, boarding house, schoolhouse and a farm."(NOTE: An interesting aside – there is an N.O. Pauly listed as living in St. Louis at this time,) In 1880, John G. Wolff was 14 and lived in Sears, Sierra County, with his father, his mother Elizabeth Wolff, who was from Louisiana, and his sisters Carrie Wolff 18; Mary Wolff, 11; Lizzie Wolff 9; and Kate Wolff, 3, In 1900, John Wolff lived in Butte, Sierra County, at a boarding house. He was working as a gold miner. Other residents at the boarding house included Camptonvillians James E. Deal and John Deal. In 1910, John Wolff lived on Railroad Avenue in Nevada City with his brother Andrew and their mother Elizabeth. He was an employee in a gold mine. In 1920 he was living in Downieville with his brother Andrew, and they were both working in their own gold mine, probably the Snowdon Hill Mine. He died sometime between 1920 and 1930. *(Sources: US Federal Census; https://thevelvetrocket.com/2012/01/25/california-ghost-towns-st-louis/; Gudde, Erwin G., California Gold Camps: University of California Press, 2009)*

WOLFF, ANDREW JACKSON "ANDY"

Andrew Jackson Wolff was born March 13, 1882 in California. His father Jean Wolff was from France, while his mother Elizabeth was from Louisiana. He had several sisters and one brother, John G. Wolff, with whom he worked the Snowdon Hill Mine. In 1920, Andrew lived with his brother in Downieville working their own gold mine. In 1930, he lived alone on Long Street in Nevada City and was a wage earner in a gold mine working as a "machine man." On his World War I draft card, he listed his address as Factory Street in Nevada City, his brother John as his nearest relative, and stated he worked in Camptonville. He died on August 10, 1931, in Nevada County and is buried in Grass Valley. *(Sources: US Federal Census; California Death Index; US World War I Draft Registration Cards*

LIST OF ILLUSTRATIONS

Page 10 Acton and "Dado" on Main Street, Camptonville, California. Leland Pauly Collection. Camptonville Historical Society.

Page 13 Brochure for White's Hospital 1912, Sacramento, California. http://cdm15248.contentdm.oclc.org/cdm/ref/collection/p15248coll3/id/1042

Page 14 White's Hospital, Sacramento, California. http://cdm15248.contentdm.oclc.org/cdm/ref/collection/p15248coll3/id/1042

Page 15 Camptonville School, 1901. Leland Pauly Collection. Camptonville Historical Society.

Page 21 Wayman accident newspaper headline. California Digital Newspaper Collection. https://cdnc.ucr.edu/cgi-bin/cdnc

Page 23 Meek Mercantile in snow, 1921. Clayton Smith Collection. Camptonville Historical Society.

Page 31 Meek Mercantile. Clayton Smith Collection. Camptonville Historical Society.

Page 36 Clark salesman car for Pacific Coast Syrup Company circa 1930
https://www.escofoods.com/about-us.html

Page 37 Buckeye Flour Mills, Yuba City, California. http://archives.csuchico.edu/cdm/ref/collection/coll11/id/19709

Page 37 Advertisement for Phoenix Gold Dust Flour. http://archives.csuchico.edu/cdm/ref/collection/coll11/id/19709

Page 41 Tom Byrd, Leland Pauly Collection

Page 42 Camptonville Brass Band. Leland Pauly Collection. Camptonville Historical Society.

Page 45 Dave Lewis, 1921. Clayton Smith Collection. Camptonville Historical Society.

Page 46 Advertisement for Hupmobile. https://www.floridamemory.com/FMP/selected_documents/large/slr_r310w-1915_04_01.jpg

Page 47 Advertisement for "Tiz" http://onehundredyearsago.blogspot.com/2015/02/the-cambria-daily-leader-23rd-february.html

Page 48 Portrait of W.B. Meek. Murphy's Old Timers Museum. http://murphysoldtimersmuseum.com/ecv/

Page 49 The Mayo Building. Photo by Stephanie Korney.

Page 57 Young Dr. Lord. Courtesy of Rosemary Wimmer.

Page 59 Dr. Lord in Uniform, World War I. Courtesy of Rosemary Wimmer.

Page 61 Members of the Crystal Truth Club. Clayton Smith Collection. Camptonville Historical Society.

Page 65 Methodist Church, Camptonville, California. Leland Pauly Collection.

Page 65 St. Francis Cabrini Church, Camptonville, California. Leland Pauly Collection.

Page 69 Old Courthouse Building, Marysville, California. http://courthousehistory.com/gallery/states/california/counties/yuba

Page 70 Judge Acton Cleveland. Leland Pauly Collection. Camptonville Historical Society.

Page 72 Dan Sharp. Clayton Smith Collection. Camptonville Historical Society.

Page 86 Andrew and Jack Wolff and workers at Snowden Mine. Ancestry.com Public Member Photos. Courtesy of John McCartney. Ancestry.com.

Page 95 Dr. James Holmes Barr. Clayton Smith Collection. Camptonville Historical Society.

Page 96 Beer glass from Billy Ward's saloon, The Grotto.. Pre-Pro.com database. http://www.pre-pro.com/midacore/view_vendor.php?vid=MSV16212

Page 102 John Edward Deal. Public Member Photos. Ancestry.com.

Page 121 Nathan Dorhmann Company. San Francisco Public Library. http://sflib1.sfpl.org:82/record=b1022122

LIST OF RESOURCES

"100 Years Ago" Nevada County Union https://www.theunion.com/news/ local-news/100-years-ago-in-nevada-county-november-1914

"Battle of Buffington Island" Wikipedia, https://en.wikipedia.org/wiki/Battle_of_Buffington_Island

"Carriage Collection." Long Island Museum. http://www.aaqeastend.com/contents/portfolio/long-island-museum-carriage-collection-finest-collection-of-horse-drawn-vehicles/;

"Ghost Towns: St. Louis," The Velvet Rocket, https://thevelvetrocket.com/2012/01/25/california-ghost-towns-st-louis/

"International Order of Good Templars," https://en.wikipedia.org/wiki/International_Organisation_of_Good_Templars

"Late Happenings Along The Coast Interesting Items of News From Those States that Border the Broad Pacific. Current Events Among Your Neighbors In the Far West Gathered by Mail and Telegraph and Presented In Kaledioscopic Array." Lompoc Journal, Number 36, 25 January 1908.

A Memorial and Biographical History of Northern California, Illustrated: Containing a History of this Important Section of the Pacific Coast from the Earliest Period of Its Occupancy...and Biographical Mention of Many of Its Most Eminent Pioneers and Also of Prominent Citizens of Today. Lewis Publishing Company,1891,California;

California County Birth, Marriage, and Death Records, 1849-1980)

California Death Index, 1905-1939

California Death Index, 1940-1997

California Historical Quarterly, Vol. 28, No. 3, Sep., 1949

California Military Registers 1858-1923

California State Court Naturalization Records 1850-1986

California Voter Registrations 1900-1968

California, County Birth, Marriage, Death Records, 1849-1980
.

California, Death Index, 1940-1997

California, Death Index, 1940-1997

California, Voter Registers, 1866-1898

California, Voter Registrations, 1900-1968

California, Wills and Probate Records, 1850-1953

Camptonville Cemetery Records; Camptonville Historical Society database.

Chamberlain, William Henry, and Wells, Harry Laurenz. *History of Yuba County, California, with illustrations descriptive of its scenery, residences, public buildings, fine blocks and manufactories.* Thompson and West Publishers, 1874.

Confederate Kentucky Volunteers War 1861-65 Records

Database of pre-Prohibition liquor distributors and

establishments. Retrieved from Pre-Pro.com http://www.pre-pro.com/index.htm

Delay, Peter, History of Yuba and Sutter Counties with Biographical Sketches OF The Leading Men and Women of the Counties Who Have Been Identified with Their Growth and Development from the Early Days to the Present, Historic Record Company, Los Angeles, California, 1924. Retrieved from http://www.archive.org/details/historyofyubasut00dela

Dyer, Steve. "Judge Acton Cleveland To Retire; Court To Close," Judges, Marshals and Constables Magazine, Judges, Marshalls, and Constables Association, Vol 32, No. 1, March 1977, pp. 1-3

Encyclopedia of American Biography, 1800-1902;
Esco website. Information retrieved from https://www.escofoods.com/about-us.html

Family stories and photos shared at ancestry.com by nolan1928, originally shared this on 15 June 2012.

Find A Grave Index, 1600s-Current

Gabriel Moulin (1872-1945); San Francisco History Center San Francisco Public Library_)

Gudde, Erwin G., California Gold Camps: University of California Press, 2009

Henness Pass Road Tour Guide

Labadie biography. Ancestry.com/cagha/biographies/l/labadie-francis.txt

Lipp & Sullivan website http://www.lippandsullivan.com/

Lord, Otho, Privately published biographical notes,1993

Mariposa Gazette, Number 32, 13 January 1917

Marysville Appeal-Democrat, January 27, 1936

Marysville Daily Appeal. November 24, 1876

McGuire, Bonnie Wayne, "The Good Judge Acton Cleveland." Used with permission of the author. Retrieved from http://www.mcguiresplace.net/The%20Laws-The%20Good%20Judge/

Meals, Hank, The Camptonville Connection: A Conversation with Leland Pauly, Tahoe National Forest, 1994.

Mill Valley Record, Volume XLIV, Number 18, 6 March 1942

Morning Press, Volume 43, Number 312, 24 December 1915

Morning Union, 2 September 1915

Morning Union, Nevada City, 1 February 1913

Morning Union, Nevada City, 1 July 1915

Morning Union, Volume 35, Number 4545, 21 October 1884

Moses Dwight Gage photo 1912, ttps://www.ancestry.com/mediaui- viewer/tree/6863521/person/6020294258/ media/af8ea6e3-5451-43d9-8dd0-de01b3805b3d?_ phsrc=DNr10&_phstart=success

Nevada City Union, June, 1911

New York Arrivals; 1860-1939

.

New York, Passenger Lists, 1820-1957

North America Family Histories, 1500-2000; The Parlin genealogy. The descendants of Nicholas Parlin of Cambridge, Mass by Frank Edson Parlin

Ogden Standard-Examiner/ Sunday, May 25, 1930

Pauly, Paul. Interview recorded in Camptonville, California, September 4. 2017. Camptonville Historical Society

Pennsylvania, Federal Naturalization Records, 1795-1931

Press Democrat, Volume XLV, Number 137, 28 September 1918;

Report of the US Civil War Solider Records

RootsWeb, Retrieved from http://www.rootsweb.com

Sacramento Bee October 23, 1903

Sacramento Bee, January 24,1936

Sacramento Bee, October 23, 1903

Sacramento Union, May 14, 1915

Sacramento Union, Number 118, 26 October 1913

Sacramento Union, Number 143, 15 January 1908

Sacramento Union, Number 24, 17 March 1906

Sacramento Union, Number 37, 6 April 1920

Sacramento Union, Number 41, 3 April 1911

Sacramento Union, Number 50, 19 August 1911

Sacramento Union, Number 54, 16 April 1906

Sacramento Union, Number 54, 24 December 1915

Sacramento Union, Number 78, 11 May 1907

Sacramento Union, Number 8, 1 September 1907

Sacramento Union, Number 9, 9 July 1919

San Mateo Times, Sep 23, 1939, p. 7
Santa Cruz Evening News, Volume 31, Number 55, 5 January 1923

Sutter County Farmers Newspaper, December 13, 1901

United States Civil War Draft Registrations Records, 1863-1865.

United States Civil War Soldier Records and Profiles, 1861-1865

United States Federal Census 1850, 1860, 1860, 1880, 1900, 1910, 1920,1930, 194

United States Find A Grave Index, 1600s-Current

United States French Catholic Church Records (Drouin Collection), 1695-1954

United States Social Security Applications and Claims Index, 1936-200

United States Social Security Death Index, 1935-2014

United States World War I Draft Registration Cards 1917-1918

United States World War I Draft Registration Cards, 1917-1918

White Hospital Brochure, Sacramento Room, Sacramento Public Library

World War II Draft Cards Young Men, 1940-1947

YubaRoots http://www.yubaroots.com;

NOTES ON THE MANUSCRIPT

This book combines three separate versions of Acton's writings.. Many of the original pages were duplicates, many had portions scratched out, and the order of their presentation was different in each version. Spelling was punctuation were erratic. In editing the manuscript, I've tried to merge the pages retaining Acton's language and the page order when it was obvious, but also re-ordering some portions when it seemed appropriate. I also tried to standardize spelling and altered punctuation for the sake of clarity. The language is all Acton's, however, and might cause some discomfort in modern readers. As the memoir is a reflection of Acton's particular time and personality, I've let it stand. To the original manuscript, I've added short biographies of most of the people mentioned in the memoir and included some additional information about places and businesses to provide a broader picture of life in Camptonville during Acton's time. I've tried to be as accurate as possible, changing the spelling of places and names when warranted through my research, but if mistakes have been made, the responsibility is mine.

Stephanie Korney, 2018

THE CAMPTONVILLE HISTORICAL SOCIETY

The Camptonville Historical Society is a nonprofit public benefit corporation. The specific purposes for which the corporation has organized are preservation of historical documents and artifacts and promotion of interest in the history of the greater Camptonville area through the vreations and sponsorship of publications, museum exhibits, and events.

To contact the society, write to Camptonville Historical Society, PO Box 153, Camptonville, CA 95922 or email info@camptonvillehistoricalsociety.org.

Made in the USA
San Bernardino, CA
08 January 2019